D1084822

Martin Buber's Spirituality

Martin Buber's Spirituality

Hasidic Wisdom for Everyday Life

Kenneth Paul Kramer

ROWMAN & LITTLEFIELD PUBLISHERS, INC.
Lanham • Boulder • New York • Toronto • Plymouth, UK

Published by Rowman & Littlefield Publishers, Inc.
A wholly owned subsidiary of The Rowman & Littlefield Publishing Group, Inc.
4501 Forbes Boulevard, Suite 200, Lanham, Maryland 20706
http://www.rowmanlittlefield.com

Estover Road, PlymouthPL6 7PY, United Kingdom

British Library Cataloguing in Publication Information Available

Library of Congress Cataloging-in-Publication Data

Kramer, Kenneth, 1941–
  Martin Buber's spirituality : Hasidic wisdom for everyday life / Kenneth Paul Kramer.
    p. cm.
  Includes bibliographical references (p.   ) and index.
  ISBN 978-1-4422-1367-8 (cloth : alk. paper)—ISBN 978-1-4422-1369-2 (electronic)
  1. Spiritual life—Judaism. 2. Hasidim—Quotations. 3. Hasidism—Quotations, maxims, etc. 4. Buber, Martin, 1878–1965. I. Title.
  BM723.K73 2012
  296.7—dc23   2011029154

∞™ The paper used in this publication meets the minimum requirements of American National Standard for Information Sciences—Permanence of Paper for Printed Library Materials, ANSI/NISO Z39.48-1992.

Printed in the United States of America

This is the ultimate purpose: to let God in. But we can let him in only where we really stand, where we live, where we live a true life. If we maintain holy intercourse with the little world entrusted to us, if we help the holy spiritual substance to accomplish itself in that section of Creation in which we are living, then we are establishing, in this our place, a dwelling for the Divine Presence.

—Martin Buber

Dedication

For Mechthild Gawlick
Who turns to engage me unreservedly
On the "narrow ridge" of genuine dialogue.

Contents

Foreword

By Maurice Friedman

Kenneth Paul Kramer has written a wonderful book on Martin Buber's *The Way of Man*. He was not concerned with making Buber's book more readable, for it already is, but with enriching and extending it so that readers from many faiths and even from no faith at all would find in it a personal life way of great significance to themselves. For this purpose, Kramer has added to his study of each of the six talks a set of questions to help the readers who want to follow this path to understand its significance. For the crux of the book is its concern for the person who might find in it a way forward. Although Kramer understands why Buber gave up his own early world-denying mysticism, he has put *The Way of Man* in a class with such mystical devotional classics as *Practicing the Presence of God* and *The Cloud of Unknowing*.

Martin Buber was a world-class philosopher and scholar. He had a personal library of forty thousand books, most of which he knew with a nearly photographic memory. He did not come from a Hasidic family and he never found a *rebbe* or become a Hasid himself. Yet his first two books were on Hasidic figures—*The Tales of Rabbi Nachman* and *The Legend of the Baal Shem*. Buber had a lifelong interest in Hasidism and continued to put together Hasidic tales and to write books about Hasidism. Two of these books were *Hasidism and Modern Man* and *The Origin and Meaning of Hasidism*, both of which I translated into English from the German original. I also translated a version of *The Legend of the Baal Shem* that improved over the one that I read that brought me into my own lifetime of interest in and commitment to Hasidism years earlier.

When Martin Buber brought out a new collection of Hasidic tales in 1948, the great German-Swiss writer Hermann Hesse, who had himself been awarded a Nobel Prize in Literature, nominated Buber for the same prize, explaining in a letter to a friend that he considered Buber's *Tales of the Hasidim* an unexcelled contribution to world literature and singled out Buber himself as one of the very few wise men of his time. In this study Kenneth Kramer has given us a glimpse of this background while preserving the simplicity and beauty of *The Way of Man.*

When I agreed to write a foreword to Kenneth Kramer's study of Martin Buber's *The Way of Man According to the Teachings of Hasidism,* I never dreamed it would become the powerfully enriching book that it now is. That is because *The Way of Man,* or as Kramer now calls it *The Human Way,* is such a little book. Yet in my reading of Kenneth Kramer's book I have never felt that he has gone beyond what is appropriate and meaningful for this little treasure which I have regarded as a classic since I first read it sixty years ago. Most studies such as this do not go beyond a careful reading and interpretation of the text. Kenneth Kramer's, in contrast, draws on psychology, philosophy, literature, and a profound understanding of Martin Buber's philosophy of dialogue as well as Buber's other, larger books on Hasidism, to craft a work that is accessible and applicable to spiritual life for those of all backgrounds.

To crown all this, Professor Kramer has enriched his study with illustrations from his own life. That life in itself is a remarkable one. When I first knew Kenneth Kramer in 1967, he was a full-fledged Protestant just out of Yale University Divinity School. That was the time when he entered the Ph.D. program in Religion and Literature that I created as part of the Department of Religion at Temple University in Philadelphia. For his doctoral dissertation Kramer delved deeply into T. S. Eliot's classic *Four Quartets.* I recommended his dissertation for publication at the University of Chicago Press which had published my own first book *Martin Buber: The Life of Dialogue* in 1955. Although I was his dissertation director, the philosophy and thought of Martin Buber were in no way central in his thinking or his study. Instead he carried forward a lifelong interest in and study of T .S. Eliot, culminating in his own remarkable book *Redeeming Time: T. S. Eliot's Four Quartets.*

During this time, however, Kramer went through basic changes in his own religious affiliation. His Protestantism yielded first to Hinduism, including substantial time spent in India, then to Buddhism, Zen Buddhism, and, for many years, Catholicism and finally, to my great surprise, Martin Buber's Hasidism. (Like me, it was impossible for him to become an actual Hasid.) Kramer's interest in Martin Buber's philosophy led him to write a book in which he presented a reading of Buber's *I and Thou* that he thought would make it more accessible to the general reader. This was followed by a Buberian book on T. S. Eliot's *Four Quartets.* Despite my love of the *Quartets* and of the philosophy of Martin Buber, I had never imagined such a book. Yet I was so impressed with it that I published a review essay strongly approving this, to me quite unexpected slant on the *Quartets.*

Now, as a follow up, Kramer has written a remarkable book on Hasidic wisdom for everyday life. I can only wish this book well and hope it reaches the wide audience that it deserves and for whom it can have great meaning.

Acknowledgments

With deepest gratitude, I wish to acknowledge Martin Buber (1878–1965) for his living teaching of unreserved dialogue. What I inherit from Buber's life and work is a profound caring for how best to be fully present—openly, honestly, immediately, mutually—in this moment.

I gratefully acknowledge teachers, colleagues, friends with whom I have discussed ideas in this book, and especially my daughters, Leila and Yvonne, who have greatly encouraged me all along the way.

I am extremely grateful to Maurice Friedman, my former teacher, who first pointed me to the inestimable, life-changing value of Buber's philosophy of dialogue and whose friendship with, translations of, and writings about Buber continue to clarify Buber's liberating life-work. But not only that, some of our encounters remain true "touchstones of reality" for me.

I am deeply appreciative to Professor Pat Boni, a student of Friedman's, for her straightforward challenges and creative comments in response to a draft of this book. Her suggestions account for improvements of phrase and construction.

I am grateful to James Brown, my former student, who landscaped my language, weeded out excessive verbiage and cultivated healthy expressions in ways that make it easier for you to move more quickly toward the book's essential spiritual substance.

I appreciate the numerous students—both at San Jose State University and in private seminars—with whom I have discussed elements of each talk and whose questions, concerns, and insights find their way into the book's chapters.

I am thankful for Sheila Willey, my operatic typist, who accompanied me through numerous iterations of each chapter with her unflappable Midwestern patience, even spotting missed typos, incorrect tenses, and confusing tropes along the way. As well, I acknowledge Taylor Skillin, a self-described "slacker typist," for his finishing touches and for mixtures of music and words.

Grateful acknowledgement is made for permission to reprint excerpts from *The Way of Man According to the Teachings of Hasidism* by Martin Buber. By the permission of the Ward & Balkin Agency, Inc.

Several paragraphs in chapter 1 can be found in a slightly different form in my article "Tasting God: Martin Buber's Sweet Sacrament of Dialogue," *Horizons Journal,* 37/2 (2010): 224–245.

The core of the conclusion incorporates selected sections of my article "Praying Dialogically: Practicing Martin Buber's Secret," *Interreligious Insight,* volume 8, number 1, January 2010.

Preface

When do you find yourself in deep communion with God? What is your chief difficulty in trying to encounter God? How do you respond when someone you respect speaks about spiritual practice? Are you interested in hearing more? When are you most at ease with life's ultimate questions, even with death? This book offers you a chance to discover practical yet powerful answers to questions like these. By highlighting six spiritual practices for meeting God offered by the renowned philosopher of religion Martin Buber (1878–1965), we will discover why finding answers to these questions is not only possible but necessary for revitalizing spiritual life.

In 1948, ten years after leaving Germany to become a professor of social philosophy at Hebrew University in Jerusalem, Buber presented six talks on spirituality at a retreat in Holland. The subject of these talks, which were called "The Way of Man According to the Teachings of Hasidism," was eighteenth century Hasidic spirituality, Buber's specialty as a researcher and religious thinker. Hasidism refers to the popular communal mystical movement of East European Jewry, arising in Poland in the eighteenth century (1750–1810), which spans the spiritual wisdom of great teachers, zaddikim, in tales and stories. At once a living reality and a teaching, Hasidism emphasized that God is present and can be glimpsed in each thing and reached through each deed of loving-kindness. In these talks, Buber presents the keys of Hasidic spirituality by addressing the importance of becoming uniquely and wholly *human*. Buber told his audience that becoming the authentic human being you were created to become is "the eternal core" of Hasidic spiritual teaching and practice. This authenticity happens when one enters a unique, unreserved relationship with God. That is why the rabbi of Kotzk taught that God calls us to "be humanly holy."[1]

Coming upon Buber's little spiritual classic, *The Way of Man According to the Teachings of Hasidism,* is like discovering a painting by an early
twentieth century European master that's been packed away in storage and
forgotten. Each work embodies a serene power; yet each is in need of renova-
tion. Just as the painting needs to be reexamined, carefully documented, and
cleaned to make it suitable for public display, the language of Buber's six
talks, translated from the German, needs to be updated to apply to our time
and cultural situation. Besides using language that is somewhat foreign to a
twenty-first century reader, the original Hasidic tales themselves reflect a late
seventeenth century spiritual worldview populated by demons and angels.
Today its title "The Way of Man" *(Der Weg des Menschen)* would more
likely be translated as "The Human Way."[2] *The Way of Man* is Buber's most
succinct, most profound presentation of spiritual life and faith. In the process
of restoring Buber's talks, I have sought to preserve his glimpses into the
inestimable value of Hasidic spiritual substance.[3]

Buber's talks on this occasion focused intently on the importance of human
action, of you and I working with intention *(kavana)* to open a space for God
to enter into our lives. By letting God into our lives, we become authentically
and unreservedly human. The more one listens to, ponders, and has a dialogue
with Buber's talks, the clearer one's action-oriented focus becomes. Hasidic
spiritual teachings, Buber wrote, "can be summed up in one sentence: God
can be *beheld* in each thing and *reached* through each pure deed."[4] As Hasidic
wisdom makes clear, one need not be Jewish, or even religious in a traditional
sense, to benefit from its teachings. Echoing this expression of the penetration
of all spheres by the divine, Buber selected six interrelated spiritual practices
that he believed could help to strengthen faith, deepen compassion, and
remove barriers to God's presence.

When I say "practice," I am speaking of the active, pragmatic, embodied
dimension of the teaching-practice continuum. In fact, "practice" always
penetrates "teaching" through and through. Without "teaching," practice
loses its structure, its expression; without "practice," "teaching" remains
incomplete, unfulfilled. I hyphenate the term "teaching-practice" to indicate
Hasidism's and Buber's non-dualistic view that embodies living practices;
practice is guided by and expresses teaching.[5] These practices, which this
book will describe in detail, are (1) *heart-searching,* (2) *your particular way,*
(3) *resolution,* (4) *beginning with yourself,* (5) *turning toward others,* and
(6) *standing-here where you are.*

When I first discussed Buber's talks on *The Way of Man* with students
who were already somewhat familiar with Buber's philosophy of dialogue,
their responses indicated that of all of his writings, the spiritual wisdom
of these talks is the easiest to understand. And here's why: these talks all

revolve around the central question, *"How can we fulfill the meaning of our personal existence on earth?"* The Hasidic answer to this question is straightforward: we can do so by "hallowing the everyday." That is, by hallowing (relating to life as holy) everyday events we invite God to participate redemptively with us in our lives. For Buber, in other words, spirituality is not something that we add to life from somewhere else, nor is it something "supernatural."

It comes as no surprise that since Buber's death in 1965, spiritual alienation and our inability to discover meaningful ways of responding to it have deepened. Fewer and fewer people turn to established religious traditions and even when they do, too often they are frustrated with result-formalized rituals rather than authentic spiritual substance; unthinking adherence to tradition rather than creative expressions of Ultimate Reality. Were Buber still alive, he would undoubtedly respond to today's spiritual malnutrition as he did to the spiritual hunger of his own time, yet with an additional emphasis. The new emphasis, I believe, would underscore Hasidism's teaching-practice of the deeply regenerating connection between persons and the "absolute Person."

Here we come to a pivotal moment—the heart-center of Buber's Hasidic sensibility flows from a crucial turning in his own life, which developed as he delved more and more deeply into Hasidic tales. Whatever else this pivotal shift involved, it effected a purification of the Gnostic elements that he found in Hasidism. As Remi Braque writes, "This purification was a process that Buber himself had to undergo, in what he acknowledged as a turning point in his thought."[6]

This shift is clearly delineated by Buber in a later essay in which he distinguishes *gnosis* from *devotio*. Against a backdrop of religious traditions, *gnosis* meant, for Buber, "a knowing relationship to the divine knowing by means of an apparently never-wavering certainty of possessing in oneself sufficient divinity."[7] Buber came to realize that *gnosis* needed to become purified of itself in acts of service (*devotio*). That is: "In Hasidism, *devotio* has absorbed and overcome *gnosis*."[8] For this reason, Buber repeatedly describes Hasidism as the practice of a worldly spirituality in which the Hasid is responsible for endeavoring to draw God into the world by *hallowing* everyday situations and events as holy.

Yet what does "spirituality" really mean? And why make such a point of it?

Hasidic spirituality, for Buber, refers to the profound reciprocity between the human spirit and the divine spirit. Spirituality involves an ongoing partnership with the invisible, unprovable, insubstantial yet creatively revealing and redeeming spirit who penetrates into our lives. According to Buber, a new conscience, a dialogical spirituality arises in and between persons who reject false absolutes "to glimpse the never-vanishing appearance of the Absolute."[9] Hasidic spirituality, therefore, is not restricted to any particular religious teaching or practice, or to any belief system, or ritual behavior, but refers instead to "the realization of the Divine in the shared life [coexistence with persons]."[10]

The word "spiritual," for Buber, does not point simply to a special realm of existence, or to a heightened mode of awareness, and it cannot be fully contained in a teaching or practice no matter how profoundly understood, no matter how intensely performed. On the contrary, Buber's Hasidic spirituality refers simply, yet meaningfully, to hallowing the everyday by letting God into the world through relating to all life as holy. The created world is not an illusion, not something which must be overcome. It is created to be hallowed. As Buber eloquently says:

> *Everything created has a need to be hallowed and is capable of receiving it: all created corporality, all created urges and elemental forces of the body. Hallowing enables the body to fulfill meaning for which it was created.*[11]

Yet, hallowing is not just a subjective act within the person. It involves much more.

Buber's Hasidic spirituality is dialogical. But dialogue, for Buber, did not just mean two people talking together. By "dialogue" Buber meant mutual openness, directness, and presentness in relationship. In genuine dialogue, experiencing the other's situation makes one wholly present. "When there's a *willingness* for dialogue," Buber's friend, translator, and biographer Maurice Friedman says, "one must 'navigate' moment-by-moment. It's a listening process."[12] Although "genuine dialogue" is more than just a concept, it does embody some elementary principles. These include turning wholeheartedly toward others, being "fully" present to another, listening attentively to what is spoken, and responding responsibly without withholding yourself. At the same time, dialogue may arise from our encounter with the sunset over the ocean, from the cry of an early owl, from the grandeur of a snow-peaked mountain, or from contact with paintings, sculpture, poetry, dance, music, film, and literature, as well as from the challenges of our everyday lives.

Dialogical spirituality is unique. It embodies a transformation from self-centeredness to relationship-centeredness, from self-obsessed individuality to ever-new, genuine relationships between us and the world, us and God. Compared to other spiritual practices, dialogical spirituality is unique because it happens when we remain open to the divine presence in ever-new events, actions, or conversations. Human beings exist, for Buber, in a continuous process of becoming, actualized in each genuine engagement with others which simultaneously helps others to become fully human. Rabbi Pinhas of Koretz put it this way:

> When a man is singing and cannot lift his voice, and another comes and sings with him, another who can lift his voice, then the first will be able to lift his voice too. That is the secret of the bond between spirit and spirit.[13]

Like a chorus, dialogical spirituality manifests itself through a common bond between spirit and spirit. This bond, which Buber called "the between," or "elemental togetherness," or "vital reciprocity," expresses itself as the spirit of harmony between the two voices, a spirit greater than the sum of these voices. That common bond—the mutual indwelling of will and grace, of compassion and wisdom arising between us—is the spiritual secret.

Buber combines a deep expertise of Hasidic wisdom tales with illuminatingly relevant insights for a fulfilling life. Throughout this book, to the extent possible, Buber's spiritual practices are presented as if he is speaking them to us right now. I supplement them with questions, exemplifications, and

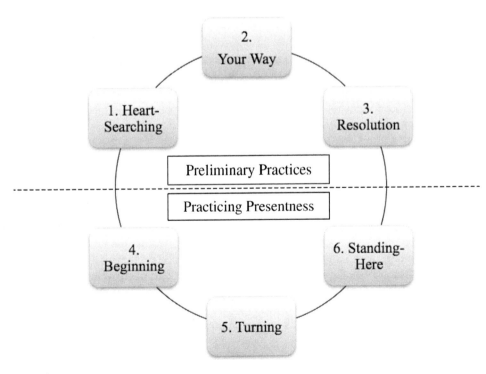

Figure 0.1

practical exercises so that you can integrate these methods into your engagement with life. To maintain and reproduce the inventive freshness of Buber's
talks while remaining true to my own dialogue with them, this book follows
the structure that Buber provided when he delivered them. His series of talks
began with a discussion of preliminary stages that prepare us for spiritual
change (chapters 1–3). He then moves to a discussion of how to participate
fully, presently, dialogically, even redemptively in life (chapters 4–6).

The first three talks speak of the need for the spiritual traveler to slow down
long enough to concentrate his or her willpower on moving ahead in dialogue.
As we retreat ahead of our habitual fears and resistance, we begin to see before
us the possibility of genuine dialogue in this present moment. That is, the preliminary practices of *heart-searching*, *your particular way*, and *resolution* set
the stage for the last three talks, our becoming fully present by *beginning with
ourselves*, *turning toward others*, and *standing-here*. Here's the point: the fulfillment of your existence, its mysterious spiritual substance, accomplishes itself
exactly where you stand in genuine relationship to living events and persons
and, simultaneously, to the Absolute. Cultivating these six spiritual practices
can help us develop as authentic human beings from a Hasidic perspective.

Comparing Buber's own titles for his talks to those used here, you can
see that the newer titles preserve Buber's original meaning. To personalize
Buber's talks, I have used "your" in place of "one" three times and in place
of "the" once. The most noticeable change occurs in chapter 5. Yet even here,
the newer title both reflects Buber's essential message in this talk and fits perfectly into his overall structure. The motive behind using newer titles was to
express Buber's Hasidic teaching-practice in ways that address and challenge
today's reader to make a unique response.

Titles of Buber's Talks

Buber's Original Titles	Newer Titles
(1) Heart-searching	(1) Heart-searching
(2) The Particular Way	(2) Your Particular Way
(3) Resolution	(3) Resolution
(4) Beginning with Oneself	(4) Beginning with Yourself
(5) Not Being Preoccupied with Oneself	(5) Turning Toward Others
(6) Here Where One Stands	(6) Here Where You Stand

To present Buber's Hasidic wisdom as clearly as possible, each chapter follows a similar six-part pattern:

(1) a one-paragraph summary of Buber's talk;

(2) the opening Hasidic tale that catalyzes Buber's commentary;

(3) a key teaching-practice for spiritual life explained;

(4) an anecdote from Buber's life that further exemplifies his main point;

(5) a closing tale which deepens Buber's commentary and points ahead to the next talk; and

(6) interrelated practice exercises designed to enrich and deepen spiritual life.

For an overview of the contents of Buber's talks, you may wish to begin this book by reading the six one-paragraph summaries at the beginning of each talk. The final sentence of each opening summary—the ridge beam supporting that talk's structure—essentializes the place where teaching and practice intersect. It might also be valuable to read other subsections, such as those discussing Buber's exemplifying life-anecdotes, consecutively. The practice exercises that conclude each chapter are collected in the appendix along with some responses to the first question in chapter one, which I've collected from my Buber seminars.

Chapter 1, "Heart-Searching," asks the question that God asked Adam and that Buber believed God asks every individual man and woman as well: "Where are you?" (in terms of your own life). Chapter 2, "Your Particular Way," answers the question "How am I to serve God?" by addressing your particular task in life, that of discovering and cultivating your own unique spiritual path. In response to the question "How can I be unified?" (become whole), Chapter 3, "Resolution," asks you to pull yourself together before attempting any significant task. Chapter 4, "Beginning with Yourself," deals with the centrally important question "What is the origin of conflict?" and suggests that the source of conflict lies within us. Chapter 5, "Turning toward Others," answers the question "What am I to unify my being for?" and offers ways for not taking oneself too seriously. In response to the question "Where does God dwell?," Chapter 6, "Here Where You Stand," speaks to what Buber saw as our ultimate purpose as humans—to let God into our lives where we stand by being fully present right here, right now. The main focus of Buber's talks, then—the divine-human relationship—is moving in measure, as T. S. Eliot said, like a dancer with our loving infinite Partner.

If you are wondering how we can know that these teaching-practices work, I can only say "try them and see for yourself." It just might happen that the six methods unpacked in this book will renew your faith, deepen your spirit, and recharge your attentiveness to whom or what you meet. See for yourself if, as Brother David Steindl-Rast has persuasively written, true spirituality results in vibrating *aliveness,* a fullness of body, mind, and spirit, and a renewed realization of our *belonging* together in common with all creation.[14]

Buber added a brief but provocative Introduction to his talks for the English translation. Since it perfectly introduces the six talks, I repeat it here verbatim.[15]

In most systems of belief the believer considers that he can achieve a perfect relationship to God by renouncing the world of the sense and overcoming his own natural being. Not so the Hasid. Certainly, 'cleaving' unto God is to him the highest aim of the human person, but to achieve it he is not required to abandon the external and internal reality of earthly being, but to affirm it in its true, God-oriented essence and thus so to transform it that he can offer it up to God.

Hasidism is no pantheism. It teaches the absolute transcendence of God, but as combined with his conditioned immanence. The world is an irradiation of God, but as it is endowed with an independence of existence and striving, it is apt, always and everywhere, to form a crust around itself. Thus, a divine spark lives in every thing and being, but each such spark is enclosed by an isolating shell. Only man can liberate it and re-join it with the Origin: by holding holy converse with the thing and using it in a holy manner, that is, so that his intention in doing so remains directed toward God's transcendence. Thus the divine immanence emerges from the exile of the 'shells.'

But also in man, in every man, is a force divine. And in man far more than in all other beings it can pervert itself, can be misused by himself. This happens if he, instead of directing it towards its origin, allows it to run directionless and seize at everything that offers itself to it; instead of hallowing passion, he makes it evil. But here, too, a way to redemption is open: he who with the entire force of his being 'turns' to God, lifts at this his point of the universe the divine immanence out of its debasement, which he has caused.

The task of man, of every man, according to Hasidic teaching, is to affirm for God's sake the world and himself and by this very means to transform both.[16]

Martin Buber

Introduction

Buber's Hasidic Spirituality

One cloudy overcast Friday, Virginia, a visiting nurse whom I had not met before, came at noon to change the pressure ulcer dressings on my ankles. Each week, for the last two months, another nurse, usually Linda, after changing each of the dressings, sat at the dining room table to enter data into her computer. Virginia did the same. She had gathered, from the books on my shelves and our conversation, that I am a retired professor of Comparative Religious Studies and that I am in the process of writing a book. At one point she looked up and said, "I was raised Catholic, but I have come to experience religion as an evil. So many bad things are done in the name of God."

"Yes," I said, "unfortunately institutional religions often split off the sacred from the ordinary—the sacred over here (in Church, in worship, in special places or activities) and the ordinary over here (in the mundane situations where life really happens). In fact, that's one of the reasons why I'm writing this book, to help overcome the spiritual fallacy of this division between the sacred and the ordinary."

"What's the book about?" she inquired, with noticeably increasing interest.

"It's about Hasidic spirituality in Buber's little classic, *The Way of Man*, which today would be translated *The Human Way*. It's about how we respond to God's question 'Where are you in the world?'"

"I don't have a relationship with God," she said. "I spent time in various churches and even some time in connection with a religious community like the Franciscans. But it never took hold."

"That's very understandable," I said. "Religious teachings and practices, rules and regulations often make it more difficult to relate to God, often get in the way of that relationship. That's partly why, after retiring from twenty-five years of teaching and simultaneously from twenty-five years of practicing Catholicism, I wanted to write this book."

"What are you now?" she asked.

"Just a human being, a faithful person living in an ongoing partnership with God. But while I pray to God as 'Heavenly Father' because of the imprint of my early religious training, I recognize that God is genderless and nameless. The Muslims have it right. In the *Qur'an* it is said that God has ninety-nine names or attributes but that God's true name is the hundredth. And no one knows that name. Just as God is beyond any name, description, definition, or imagining."

"For me," she said, "I respect the earth and try to live responsibly here and now."

"There it is. That's where God is present for you. God is unique to each person."

"Mmm . . ."

"For me, it's a faith commitment. I experience being called into a dialogical partnership with the nameless Eternal Partner who is revealed in ever-unique, ever-surprising ways."

"Where can I read about this way of thinking?" she asked. "I've never heard anything like this in church."

"One place most certainly is in the stories and teachings of Hasidism . . ."

"You mean the fundamentalists with dreadlocks?" she asked with surprise.

"No, the eighteenth-century Eastern European communal mystical movement in Jewish ghettos which has since died out. Its stories have been collected and retold by Martin Buber, stories about the sacramentality of everyday life. One of the best places to begin reading about Hasidic teaching is his little classic *The Way of Man According to the Teachings of Hasidism*. These six talks were given to people attending a spiritual retreat. It's as if Buber took off his coat jacket, rolled up his shirt sleeves, and spoke in simpler language than he does elsewhere." I include this brief interaction because it duplicates other exchanges I've had about the significance of Buber's Hasidic spirituality. Yet before beginning our discussion of these teachings, it would be helpful to know something about Martin Buber the person. Who is he?

WHY BUBER?

Why is it important in the twenty-first century to study the religious philosophy of Martin Buber, who wrote in the last century? Buber is a Jewish philosopher of religion who has been acknowledged as one of the greatest thinkers of the twentieth century, comparable to Gandhi, Albert Schweitzer, and Einstein, and who was nominated for a Nobel Prize in literature by Dag Hammarskjöld, former secretary general of the United Nations. Hermann Hesse also nominated Buber for the Nobel Prize in literature, saying that Buber was one of the few wise men living in the world today, a writer of a very high order who has enriched world literature with his Hasidic tales. Called by his American biographer Maurice Friedman one of the "universal geniuses of our time," Buber stands among the most significant religious philosophers of the twentieth century.[1]

Buber was an extraordinary human being. While one needs to know at least three or four languages (ancient and modern) to completely understand his writings, only the language of humanity is necessary to understand his being. He was so full of life from within that an effervescence shone through his face. When Friedman first met Buber in a New York hotel (Buber was staying there while teaching at the Jewish Theological Seminary), Buber welcomed him by looking deeply into his eyes while taking his hand. Friedman's initial response was to feel how totally "other" Buber seemed. His eyes were of a depth, gentleness, and directness that Friedman had never before, or since, encountered. Indeed, in 1961, a year after Friedman had spent four months in Jerusalem with Buber, he asked himself, "What did I experience when I looked into Buber's eyes?"[2] Friedman realized that Buber really included him and thereby placed a demand on him to be fully present. In even more descriptive language, Buber's friend Aubrey Hodes writes that Buber's eyes were "grey, proud, secure, tender, near."[3]

What sets Buber apart from most contemporary spiritual thinkers is that Buber has placed "genuine dialogue"—direct, honest, open, spontaneous, mutual communication—at the center of the soul's search for God. In that light, Buber characterized his own spiritual position in relation to others and to God as that of one standing on the insecure "narrow ridge" between the sacred and the everyday. On this narrow-ridge, in which there is no certainty of expressible knowledge, a space opens where the meeting between God and humans occurs.

In the last years of his life, a biblical scholar asked Buber whether he held his translation of the Bible and his biblical studies to be the quintessence of his life work. Buber replied:

If I myself should designate something as the "central portion of my life work," then it could not be anything individual, but only the one basic insight that has led me not only to the study of the Bible, as to the study of Hasidism, but also to an independent philosophical presentation: that the I-Thou relation to God and the I-Thou relation to one's fellow [hu]man are at bottom related to each other. This being related to each other is . . . the central portion of the dialogical reality that has ever more disclosed itself to me.[4]

Considering the wide-ranging subject matter of Buber's thought (he wrote and spoke about Taoism, Hasidism, mysticism, dialogue, education, psychotherapy, ethics, religion, Judaism, Christianity, and more), and in light of all his awards, recognitions, and achievements, when Buber says that one basic insight guided him in all his work, we should naturally pay close attention to what this insight was.

Buber's basic insight is that God's ever-new, ever-loving presence appears to us in life itself. Buber characterized genuine, unreserved dialogue as a sacramental act, which embodies and expresses the covenant between humans and the absolute, between the human "I" and the divine "Thou." Genuine dialogue, for Buber, occurs on the "narrow ridge" between absolute truths, between dualisms of life and death, good and bad, God and the world. As Buber once remarked:

> *I do not accept any absolute formulas for living . . . No preconceived code can see ahead to everything that can happen in a [person's] life. As we live, we grow, and our beliefs change. They must change. So I think we could live with this constant discovery. We should be open to this adventure in heightened awareness of living. We should stake our whole existence on our willingness to explore and experience.*[5]

There, on the narrow ridge, if we become attuned to listening, we can hear three voices, not just two, in every genuine dialogue: mine, yours, and the voice of relationship itself.

Buber called his own dialogical faith "Hebrew humanism," or "believing humanism." In Buber's understanding, faith and humanity:

> *do not appear as two separate realms each of which stands under its own signs and under its special laws: they penetrate each other, they work together; indeed, they are so centrally related to each other that we may say our faith has our humanity as its foundation, and our humanity has our faith as its foundation.*[6]

How simple, how profound: faith that God is present in this very moment penetrates and informs our humanness, and unreserved, spontaneous humanness penetrates our faith. In Buber's last years, he often spoke about this kind of humanism, which he called "faithful," "devout," or "believing." Aubrey Hodes once said to Buber, "What you are speaking about is Hasidism permeated by humanist ideals, humanism permeated by Hasidic fervor. In short, a Hasidic humanism." Hodes reports that Buber responded "Yes, I think that is very near. . . . A humanist who acts with *hesed,* with loving-kindness."[7] Buber's believing or Hasidic humanism offers a liberating alternative to the seemingly endless disconnections, breakdowns, and distresses of contemporary culture. Indeed, I turn to Buber with the conviction, based on experience, that the method of genuine dialogue brings attitude-changing results to human relationships.

Though he is often called a "philosophical anthropologist" or a "religious existentialist," Buber was by his own definition a *Schriftsteller*, both a writer and one who renders scriptures. Philosophy, sociology, and religion all played into his world-view, but throughout his later writings in particular Buber strove to simply point the way to the life of dialogue. Indeed, toward the end of his life, when asked if he was a theologian or a philosopher, Buber responded:

> *I must say it once again: I have no teaching. I only point to something . . . I point to something in reality that had not or had too little been seen. I take him who listens to me by the hand and lead him to the window. I open the window and point to what is outside. I have no teaching, but I carry on a conversation.*[8]

Buber's "basic insight" is that genuine interhuman encounters and our encounters with God are deeply bonded and mutually reciprocal. Looking out the window onto the world from this perspective opens a space for God's creative presence to penetrate your life, for God to become dialogically perceivable.

In this spirit, Buber's presentation of Hasidic spirituality (1) *points* me to the redemptive significance of human experiences which, though common to us all, often go unnoticed, (2) *opens* my heart and mind to an interactive vision for becoming fully human, (3) *reminds* me, without dogmatism, of the always-present mutuality between God and myself, and (4) *helps* me to excavate the fullness of existence that, over time, becomes buried like a treasure under layers of ignorance, laziness, forgetfulness, and habit. What all this finally comes to is simple and direct: the fulfillment of existence—our human birthright—can be found right here in the midst of genuine relationships.

Why Buber? Because, as Jacob Trapp writes:

> Even in Martin Buber's most scholarly and difficult works, there is scarcely a page that is not lit up with some rare intuitive and illuminating insight. A light from beyond seems suddenly to break through, and the ineffable seems somehow to clothe itself in words and to reveal a meaning.[9]

WHY HASIDISM?

For more than 30 years, I've studied, practiced, and taught the spiritual practices of the great religious traditions of the East and West. When asked, today, which tradition I favor, my response at this stage of my life is, "eighteenth century Hasidism as popularized by the philosopher of religion Martin Buber."[10] The word Hasidism is derived from the Hebrew word *Hasidut*, which means allegiance and piety and is derived, in turn, from the noun *hesed,* which means loving kindness, mercy, or grace. As Buber wrote in a brief poem entitled, "Hasidut":

Near to heaven, near to the bustle of earth—
Therefore I translate it: love for everything living.[11]

In this spirit, Buber viewed the Hasidic spiritual movement as a renewal of authentic Jewish life.[12] How? In what way? Buber distinguishes between *religiosity* (a creative, dynamic, living relationship to God in the present moment) and *religion* (institutionalized, rule-bound acceptance of teachings passed down through the ages without questioning). Authentic religiosity brings us into a life-renewing connection with the ever-present God. In this context, Buber pointed to the vital religiosity present in Hasidism. Here's Buber's main point: he wanted to open eyes/ears to the *actuality* and *authenticity* of a dialogical life—its presence—in the Hasidic movement.[13]

A reform movement within rabbinic Judaism, Hasidism was a popular, impassioned communal mysticism arising in Galacia (Eastern Poland and Western Ukraine) between 1750 and 1810, and which, despite bitter persecution at the hands of traditional rabbinism, swept through European Jewish life in the eighteenth century. The Hasidim established real communities each with its own rebbe or leader, who was also called the zaddik, the righteous person. Each zaddik had his own unique teaching that he imparted to his community. At one point Hasidism included almost half of the population in its communities. Tales that capture the spirit of this movement were transmitted orally from generation to generation and not written down until a half century later, when European Jews became afraid of losing them.

As a movement, Eastern European Hasidism saw no division between religion and ethics, or between one's direct relation to God and one's relation to others. The true Hasid (the devout one who kept faith with the covenant) hallowed (or consecrated and made holy) the everyday world. Each person was responsible for the piece of the world entrusted to him or her. This teaching of full presence in the world and full presence with God underpins the Hasidic way of being.

Readers who are somewhat familiar with Buber's early life may at first be surprised that he was so deeply attracted to Hasidic mysticism. It is well-known that Buber broke with his early interest in unitive mystical experience, examples of which he assembled in his anthology of mystical writings, *Ecstatic Confessions* (1909). In these multi-religious accounts, Buber found reports of unitive experience not in oneself but in the world-soul, or in God. In contrast to these mystics, whose ecstatic realizations attracted the young Buber, it soon became important for him to preserve each person's unique relationship to the world. Without this separation, he felt that no genuine encounter with God could occur. Buber thus became deeply influenced by the "realistic" and "active" mysticism of Hasidic teachers. In carefully delineated language, he speaks of this realistic mysticism as

- *The reality between God and humans in which reciprocity manifests itself . . .*
- *The subject of one's answering service of creation, destined to be redeemed through the meeting of the divine and human need . . .*
- *Not the unification of the soul with God, but the unification of God with His glory that dwells in the world . . .*
- *A mysticism that . . . preserves the immediacy of the relation, guards the concreteness of the absolute and demands the involvement of the whole being.*

For these reasons, he added that mysticism's *"true English name is perhaps: presentness."*[14]

What attracted Buber to Hasidism in this context was the fact that "God can be beheld in each thing and reached through each pure deed."[15] Hasidism's principal teaching is that God wants to be let into the world and that we can bring God into the world and our lives by wholly turning to the other in dialogue. Two secrets therefore intersect and interact at the heart of Hasidic spiritual life: the secret bond between human spirit and human spirit and the secret bond between God's "absolute transcendence" and "conditioned immanence." When these two secrets, so to speak, sing together, the gap between the sacred and the ordinary, between God and the world, and between this moment and all moments disappears and we glimpse God's presence in the midst of each genuine relationship. Yet, how is this described?

Every act, in Hasidic life, may become holy. According to the Hasidic account of creation, in the beginning God created and cast away many worlds before creating this one. With the breaking apart of the previous worlds, which could not bear divine fullness, the "holy sparks" fell into this world and now reside imprisoned in shells within everything and everyone awaiting release, awaiting redemption. Nothing is empty of them. It is our task through holy intention, and through wholly turning toward the other, to raise the divine sparks from their restriction into this world. Insofar as these sparks are everywhere, there is no place, no time, no event, no moment in our lives in which we can not encounter God's presence. We thus meet God not by withdrawing from every day encounters into solitude but by taking, with our whole spirit, a hallowing stance toward everything and everyone encountered. When divine sparks are liberated, God's glory emerges from its hiddenness.

Hasidism, for Buber, and the Hasidic tales that concretize its teachings, contain an implicit critique of both the contemporary crisis of alienation as well as of institutional religions. To the extent that religion is the sum total of customs and teachings, laws and dogmas, handed down through the years in an unalterable system that determines behavior, to that extent religious teachings are passively accepted and uncreative. For this reason, Buber spoke of the need for "religiosity," what I would call spirituality: the creative renewal of teachings, the wonder and adoration at the ever new presence of the Unconditioned, the always new relationship with the Absolute through everyday encounters.[16] The "highest intensity and transfiguration in religious reality," for Buber, is the every moment in which "unlimited Being becomes, as absolute person, my partner."[17]

When we consider the significance of Hasidic spirituality within the history of Jewish faith, we do not begin with its teachings. Considered by itself, Hasidic teaching contains nothing new, nothing that does not also appear in many other spiritual traditions. What constitutes its uniqueness, its greatness, for Buber, is not its teaching but its mode of life, its "living connection with this world and the world above." Hasidism did not "proceed *from* a teaching but moved *to* a teaching" such that one's "life worked as a teaching, as a teaching not yet grasped in words."[18] When a person is able to wholly affirm the world, God in turn is wholly affirmed. Therefore, it is not enough to serve God through formal ritual, important as rituals are. Rather, "each person can uncover and redeem this spark at each time and through each action, even the most ordinary, if only [one] performs it in purity, wholly directed to God and consecrated in Him."[19]

Until his fourteenth year, Buber spent his childhood on the estate of his grandfather, Solomon Buber, in Galacia, who as it happened serendipitously was a Midrash scholar. (Midrash is a term for commentary on biblical texts.) Inevitably, therefore, Buber was surrounded by scattered fragments of biblical interpretation. He saw in his grandfather a spiritual passion that manifested itself in his incessant dedication to his work. Though his grandfather often spoke Hebrew when visited by guests, his grandfather did not participate in Jewish religious life. Still, the young Buber realized that it dwelled within him. As long as Buber lived with him his roots were firm, even though questions and doubts had begun to arise. During this time, Buber's earliest encounter with Hasidism came "as a boy through half-degenerate offshoots." In them he "obtained a fleeting impression without realizing what it meant."[20]

Buber's early interest in Hasidism was ignited when his grandfather took him to religious services in the village of Sadagora. There, through the eyes of a precocious child, he witnessed the rebbe standing in silent prayer and then interpreting the mystery of Torah. When he saw the Hasidim dance with the Torah, he reports that he felt a strong personal sense of community. In

Hasidism, Buber saw a form of living community in which the self—I—is not isolated/separated from but constituted in relationship to others. As he wrote:

> *The Hasidic communal group, like all genuine community, consists of men who have a common, immediate relation to a living center, and just by virtue of this common center have an immediate relation to one another. In the midst of the Hasidic community stands the zaddik, whose function it is to help the Hasidim, as persons and as a totality, to authenticate their relation to God in the hallowing of life . . .* [21]

Until his twentieth year Buber's spirit was in constant flux. Buber's confusion and doubt led him to the point of wanting to know more about Judaism—not in an anthropological, historical, or sociological sense, but "the immediate knowing, the eye-to-eye knowing of the people in its creative primal hours."[22] At this point he began to acquire Hasidism anew. He began reading Hebrew texts voraciously, gradually overcoming the strangeness of the Hebrew language.

Buber's understanding of Hasidism was intensified and deepened with his discovery, in 1904, of *The Testament of Rabbi Israel Baal-Shem,* a collection of sayings attributed to Israel Ben Eliezer (1700–1760). Israel Ben Eliezer, the *Baal-Shem-Tov* (or "Baal-Shem," in shortened form) was honorifically known as the Master of the Good Name of God, and is attributed as the founder of the Hasidim. Not much is known about the Baal-Shem. He was born in a small village in Poland near the beginning of the eighteenth century. Although he wrote down nothing of his own teachings, legends tell that he was taught the mystical meanings of the scriptures by the prophet Ahiya of Shilo who lived at the time of Solomon. The teachings of the Baal-Shem were written by his followers who looked up to him as a God-inspired person. Buber uses the life of the Baal-Shem to bring forward a living relationship to the world that was the Rabbi's central concern.

In his twenty-sixth year, one day Buber opened a little book of the Baal-Shem-Tov. The Baal-Shem's words effected what can only be described as a conversion.

> *The words flashed towards me. "He takes unto himself the quality of fervor. He arises from sleep with fervor, for he is hallowed and become another* [person] *and he is worthy to create and is become like the Holy One, blessed be He, when He created His world." It was then that, overpowered in an instant, I experienced the Hasidic soul. The primally Jewish opened to me, flowering to newly conscious expression in the darkness of exile:* [our] *being created in the image of God I grasped as deed, as becoming, as task.* [23]

What he recognized in that moment, what was revealed was his life-long responsibility for being. Buber realized that he (along with all who are addressed by Hasidism) was summoned to become a creator in the world—indeed, a co-creator with God. Buber then recalled his childhood experiences in Sadagora and Czortkow of the zaddik and his disciples. Memories of their joyful community reawoke in him. In this overwhelming body-mind-spirit experience, Buber realized that the

> *primally Jewish reality was primal human reality, the content of human reli-*
> *giousness. Judaism as religiousness, as "piety," as Hasidut opened to me there.*
> *The image out of my childhood, the memory of the zaddik and his community,*
> *rose upward and illuminated me: I recognized the idea of the perfected [person].*
> *At the same time I became aware of the summons to proclaim it to the world.*[24]

Shortly after this breakthrough, Buber withdrew for five years into one of the most rewarding periods of his life, a period of private study and meditation during which he began collecting and reflecting upon Hasidic tales. This period generated a long series of major works on Hasidism that started from Buber's 1906 book on Rabbi Nachman and continued through his 1948 *The Way of Man* almost to the end of his life. In that light, how did Buber characterize his own spiritual position? Buber often depicted his stance, in relation to others and to God, as standing on the insecure "narrow ridge" between the sacred and the everyday. From this vantage, Buber formulated a radical third alternative, a space in which there is no certainty of expressible knowledge and where the dialogical meeting between God and human beings occurs.

More specifically, to become perfected, to release the divine sparks hidden in everyday reality, according to Hasidic teaching, one needs a helper, a counselor for both body and soul. This helper was the zaddik, the perfected person, the righteous one who stands the test. The zaddikim were leaders, teachers, and tradition-bearers whose authority arose from the lives they lived. According to Buber, such a teacher

- *takes you by the hand and guides you until you are able to venture on alone,*
- *does not relieve you of doing what you have grown strong enough to do for yourself,*
- *strengthens the Hasid in the hours of doubting,*
- *develops the Hasid's power of prayer,*
- *teaches the Hasid how to give the words of prayer the right direction, and*
- *joins his own prayer to that of his community, which lends the community courage and an increase of power.*[25]

The zaddik, the true helper or guide, was for Buber an ideal example of a holy human being. The zaddik's presence was an indispensable pivot, the center of the community of genuine dialogue. The dialogue between the zaddik and the Hasid was intertwined with the Hasid's dialogue with God.

What gives Hasidism its distinctive character is the dialogical rapport between the student (the Hasid) and the teacher (the zaddik). The zaddik, the "righteous one," helps, strengthens, and encourages the Hasid by making communication with God easier. The Hasid, "the devout," is a member of a community who keeps faith with the biblical covenant. The Hasid's life is directed toward spiritual values that are "considered more desirable than any intellectual accomplishment."[26] After discovering the Hasidic tales and the principles that lay behind them, Buber spent decades collecting, arranging, and then publishing two volumes containing thousands of Hasidic stories: *The Tales of the Hasidim: The Early Masters* and *The Tales of the Hasidim: The Later Masters* (each published originally in Hebrew in 1946).

It must be remembered that Hasidic teaching is not considered a collection of knowable principles but is inseparably united with deeds. Indeed, the power of Hasidic tales derives, in part, from the sense of immediacy that the tales evoke. At the same time, deeds without the teaching can easily lose their transcendent direction. Why Hasidism? Because it calls everyone, not only Jews, to turn towards a never-ending dialogical relationship with God by turning, simultaneously, towards concrete life-relationships with others.

In contrast to other-worldly spiritual traditions, which account for most of the world's religious faiths, Hasidic stories or legendary anecdotes are meant to ground the student in the sacredness of the everyday. According to Buber, Hasidic tales

> are called anecdotes because each one of them communicates an event complete in itself, and legendary because at the base of them lies the stammering of inspired witnesses who witness to what befell them, to what they comprehended as well as to what was incomprehensible to them; for the legitimately inspired has an honest memory that can nonetheless outstrip all imagination.[27]

Like similar Zen Buddhist, Taoist, or Sufi stories that record exchanges between the teacher and the seeker, Hasidic tales are meant to offer transformative insights right where we stand. Essential to Hasidic tales, as to Zen Buddhist *koans*, is the conviction that real awakening takes place not as a result of reading scripture or taking up a solitary practice, but in a living response to being challenged at the core of one's being. Hasidic tales have the power to reshape the way in which we relate to the world. In retelling them, Buber intended to create a dialogue with the stories that would have transforming effects for the reader/listener. He believed in the power of the stories to engage readers/listeners in an authentic (I-Thou) dialogue with the tale.

With increasing clarity and conviction Buber realized that an intellectual understanding of Hasidism alone is insufficient. As he said in 1924:

> *When I began my work on Hasidic literature my concern was with the Teaching and the Way. At the time I thought that contemplating them was permissible, but since then I learned that the Teaching exists in order to be learned and that the Way exists in order to walk therein.*[28]

Each Hasidic tale is less concerned with *what* is learned than with *how* what one learns is lived, which is why they come to us as stories rather than philosophical or theological treatises on abstract concepts. When one attentively integrates what the tale is unfolding, the dualism between the teacher and the taught and between the sacred and profane crumbles, replaced by a hallowing of relationships. Embodying this spirit of direct experience, in 1965, the year that he died, Buber wrote, "I have not been able to accept either the Bible or Hasidism as a whole; in one and in the other I had to and I have to distinguish between that which had become evident to me out of my experience as truth and that which had not become evident to me in this manner."[29]

In response to a question about the nature of God and his interpretation of Hasidism, Buber urged the questioner not to confuse his interpretation of Hasidism with his own thought: "I can by no means in my own thinking take responsibility for Hasidic ideas, although my thinking is indebted to them and bound up with them." Buber continued "Hasidism has exercised a great personal influence on me; much in it has deeply affected my own thinking, and I have felt myself called ever again to point to its value for the life of [humans]."[30]

While Buber was not a Hasid, he was captured by its fervor and therefore felt commissioned to help its *teaching-way* out into the world. It has never been my intention, Buber remarked, to describe/analyze Hasidic teaching but instead to direct attention, as much as possible, toward its "realization of [genuine] dialogue with being. . . ." As the impact of its spiritual life became more irresistible, for Buber, it became necessary "to take into my own existence as much as I actually could of what had been truly exemplified for me there."[31]

WHY *THIS BOOK?*

In an era when many of us find ourselves habitually behind computer and TV screens for news and entertainment, endlessly confronted with visual and audio stimuli, we may find it challenging to discover any truly meaningful relationship with God. There is, it seems to me, an increasing hunger for examples of personal and relational spirituality. Martin Buber's little classic *The Way of Man According to the Teachings of Hasidism* addresses this hunger. Of all of Buber's writings, philosophical or biblical, Hasidic or literary, these talks are unique in their presentation of Hasidic faith. In them, Buber distills the quintessence of spiritual teachings from a wealth of Hasidic stories. Buber selects six legendary anecdotes then applies their practices to spiritual life. Each of the anecdotes illustrates the importance of one of the following Hasidic dispositions: *Heart-Searching, Your Particular Way, Resolution, Beginning with Yourself, Turning Toward Others,* and *Standing-Here.*

Here are one-sentence summaries of Buber's six retreat talks in which Hasidic spiritual teachings and practices reanimate each other.

1: *HEART-SEARCHING*

Decisive heart-searching—the beginning of the human way—happens again and again when you whole-heartedly face the Voice and respond to God's question "Where are you?," which is designated to destroy your system of hideouts and to help you know whence you came, where you are going, and to whom you will have to render accounts.

2: *YOUR PARTICULAR WAY*

To properly serve God, every person's unique task is precisely to get in touch with life by hallowing (sanctifying everyday things and moments) your relationships with others and with God in your own way and with your whole being.

3: *RESOLUTION*

Before undertaking any spiritual practice, it is necessary to be resolved to unify your soul, to straighten yourself out by refocusing on the goal and by remaining wholly open to whatever addresses you in partnership with the Divine Presence.

4: *BEGINNING WITH YOURSELF*

To advance spiritually, you must begin with yourself, not with the trivial ego but with the deeper self, by taking full responsibility for any conflict-situations, by harmonizing your thought, speech, and action, and by saying what you mean and doing what you say.

5: *TURNING* TOWARD OTHERS

Practicing genuine turning, from self-orientation toward the otherness of the other, for Buber both renews you from within and deepens your relationship with God in the world.

6: *STANDING-HERE*

The fulfillment of existence, discovering the ultimate purpose for which you were created—letting God into your life—occurs when you establish a dwelling place for the Divine Presence by maintaining holy interaction with the world right here and now where you are standing and where you live.

Like Brother Lawrence's *Practicing the Presence of God,* or Julian of Norwich's *Showings,* or the anonymous author's *Cloud of Unknowing,* Buber's presentation of Hasidic mystical teachings can serve as a guide to the spiritual life to those both within and without the Hasidic tradition. Yet how, you might be asking, can we really engage Buber's words or the Hasidic tales themselves, since Buber and the eighteenth century Hasidic rabbis are no longer alive?

First, we need to catch ourselves in our daily routines, pause for a moment, step back and slow down. To escape the alienation of our lives, we need, in the words of the French critic Roland Barthes, "to retreat ahead of it."[32] The term "retreat" usually indicates taking time away from one's ordinary activities to clear away distractions and to cultivate a new sensibility. Perhaps you've already been hearing a small but persistent interior voice encouraging you to step back and ponder the direction that your life is taking. Taking time off from one's normal activities is necessary to opening a space for clearing away the old and cultivating the new. The purpose of "making a retreat," of spending time apart in an environment stripped of distractions, is to concentrate on cutting through whatever prevents us from cultivating new spiritual habits. It may even be that we spend too much time seeking God and not enough time listening for God's voice in our lives.

To retreat, then, provides an opportunity for meeting God. We need not take a retreat far from home. Instead, by willingly and consciously finding for ourselves a time and place in which to retreat with some constancy, we can accomplish soul-transformation. In this spirit, readers may read this book as if going on a spiritual retreat in which you read and ponder Buber's teaching of Hasidic spirituality without distractions, respond to the exercises, and then *bring your responses into dialogue with others.*

Second, we can take Buber's advice into account. Buber once suggested that when reading words of a dead master we treat the text not as data but as the living voice of the author. We can enter into a meaningful dialogue with a text, and by making its words immediately present, by hearing the voice of the speaker. As the Maggid of Mezritch once said to his disciples:

> I shall teach you the best way to say [or read] Torah. You must cease to be aware of yourselves. You must be nothing but an ear which hears what the universe of the word is constantly saying within you. The moment you start hearing what you yourself are saying you must stop.[33]

When a text becomes a living presence, for us readers-as-hearers, we enter into conversation with the author's voice. A Hasidic story, or any story for that matter, makes no impact on me as long as it remains a mere presentation of ideas or a description of events. But when I read dialogically, I *hear* the Voice addressing me, I recognize who is speaking to me, and I respond directly and honestly to the text from where I stand. Reading slowly and more mindfully is like becoming acquainted with another person. Better yet, it's like having a genuine dialogue with a friend in which each person is renewed.

T. S. Eliot, who met Buber in London in 1951, and who said that he had the rare experience of being in "the presence of greatness," spoke in a similar manner about reading devotional literature. In a preface to an anthology of spiritual texts, Eliot claimed that very few people really know how to read these texts. Spiritual reading, he wrote, "is the most difficult of all, because it requires an application not only of the mind, not only of the sensibility, but of the whole being." Moreover, after affirming the importance of examining the work as a whole, Eliot wrote of the need to "read two or three passages (at first, choosing passages in the same section), to attend closely to every word, to ponder on the quotations read for a little while and try to fix them in [your] mind, so that they may continue to affect [you] while [your] attention is engrossed with the affairs of the day."[34]

Third, just as Buber brought his own stand into dialogue with the Hasidic tradition, refusing to swallow it whole while embracing his profound indebtedness to its teachings, Buber would encourage us to engage his own words dialogically. For this reason, I have added breakthrough practice exercises at the conclusion of each chapter that encourage dialogue, with oneself and with others, about the key concepts Buber presents. These exercises are of three kinds: (1) they contain chapter-specific questions designed to bring greater clarity to Buber's central insights; (2) they contain comparative questions designed to deepen your dialogue with Buber's spiritual practices; and (3) they contain feedback questions designed to help you achieve life-integrations in meaningful dialogue with others.

These questions are not intended as an end in themselves, but as a starting-point for further engagement with spiritual life. You may wish to record your responses to these questions in a retreat journal. Keeping a journal facilitates further reflection and often becomes a resource for future dialogues. A fuller description of the journal process, a complete list of the thirty-two questions used throughout the book, and examples of selected responses to the personal, deeply existential question God asks everyone—"Where are you?"—can be found in the appendix.

Part I

Preliminary Practices

Chapter 1

Heart-Searching

"The decisive heart-searching is . . . again and again, the beginning of a human way." (134–35)

SUMMARY OF BUBER'S FIRST TALK

Buber begins his first talk, "Heart-Searching," with a Hasidic anecdote, as he also will in the five that follow. Buber sets this talk in the context of the first dialogical encounter between God and Adam as related in the Book of Genesis. God's first words to Adam after he eats from the Tree of Knowledge are "Where are you?" Hasidic teaching personalizes this question: God asks it of everyone in every moment, and dialogue depends upon responding to this question in a way that brings you into a deeper relationship with the world. For Buber, the key to this story is the deep bond of relationship it implies between the divine and human, Adam and God. Buber says that, like Adam, each person hides from God, but that in hiding from God each person also hides from him- or herself. God's question asks us to reveal honestly where we are hiding from the divine voice, to search our hearts and respond honestly about where we stand. God does not ask us to pursue a sterile heart-searching of sin and self-condemnation, however. Instead of that, God asks for a decisive answer from the real ground of our being. Essentially, decisive heart-searching—the beginning of the human way—happens again and again when you wholeheartedly face the Voice and respond to God's question "Where are you?," which is designated to destroy your system of hideouts and to help you know whence you came, where you are going, and to whom you will have to render accounts.

3

OPENING HASIDIC TALE

Rabbi Shneur Zalman, the rav [rabbi] *of Northern White Russia (died 1813), was put in jail in Petersburg, because the mitnagdim* [adversaries of Hasidism] *had denounced his principles and his way of living to the government. He was awaiting trial when the chief of the gendarmes entered his cell. The majestic and quiet face of the rav, who was so deep in meditation that he did not at first notice his visitor, suggested to the chief, a thoughtful person, what manner of man he had before him. He began to converse with his prisoner and brought up a number of questions which had occurred to him in reading the Scriptures. Finally he asked: 'How are we to understand that God, the all-knowing, said to Adam: "Where art thou?"'*

'Do you believe,' answered the rav, 'that the Scriptures are eternal and that every era, every generation and every man is included in them?'

'I believe this,' said the other.

'Well then,' said the zaddik, 'in every era, God calls to every man: "Where are you in your world? So many years and days of those allotted to you have passed, and how far have you gotten in your world?" God says something like this: "You have lived forty-six years. How far along are you?"'

When the chief of the gendarmes heard his age mentioned, he pulled himself together, laid his hand on the rav's shoulder, and cried: 'Bravo!' But his heart trembled. (130-1)

KEY TEACHINGS AND PRACTICES

The first practice that can move us toward genuine dialogue with the world and with God is to find and offer a heart-searching response to God's question. Heart-searching does not mean, for Buber, just checking to see how you feel, though it includes that. It also means deeply pondering your whole self and trying to understand where you are in this moment. It is important, therefore, that God's question "Where are you?" reaches from your mind down into your heart. It is not enough for the question to remain an idea in your head. It is essential that God's question is transported to the heart of our body, mind, and spirit. You must hear the question with the ears of your heart, so to speak, and respond to it with your heart's voice.

This first spiritual practice, upon which the others depend for support and from which they take their direction, happens as the result of a co-creative partnership between us and God. It is for the sake of this divine-human relationship that God asks the question in the first place, and it is the dynamic interaction of this partnership itself that enables you to really hear, face, and respond to God's question. Indeed, the basic insight of Buber's life work—that the relationship between person and person and between person and God, when genuine, is deeply bonded—fuels this first practice and fuels the other five practices as well. It is for this reason that whatever else prayer may be, for Buber it is always God's presence becoming "dialogically perceivable."

In Buber's spiritual wisdom, relationship—when it is genuine, mutual, open, and present—is our birthright as human beings. "In the beginning is relationship," he wrote. The shift from the head to heart is a shift from knowing, thinking, describing, and objectifying to affirming, answering, and relating. Genuine heart-searching brings our initial responses into dialogue with those who are also interested in God's question. True understanding, true decision-making, for Buber, occurs in dialogical interactions in which our limited self-understanding is questioned, challenged, and either reshaped or affirmed. The ultimate goal, according to Buber, is not just to put the mind in the heart, but to bring your heart, mind, body, and spirit into relationship.

GOD'S QUESTION

What happens, then, in this Hasidic tale, which opens the first of Buber's retreat talks? Rabbi Schneur Zalman, a Hasid who has been imprisoned because of his principles and his way of living, is in deep meditation when he is suddenly questioned by the jailer: Why did God, the all-knowing, say to Adam: "Where are you?"

In response, the rav said: "Do you believe that the Scriptures are eternal and that every era, every generation and every [person] is included in them?"

"I believe this," said the jailer.

"Well then" said the zaddik, "in every era, God calls to every person: 'where are you in your world?'"

When the jailer replies "Bravo," his heart trembles because the rabbi's reply spoke directly and profoundly to the jailer's existential situation. The ancient rabbis understood God's question "Where are you in your world" to mean a few different things: (1) "How far along are you in your life?" (2) "How far along are you in your readiness to acknowledge God?" (3) "How far along are you in making your life *worthy*?" With this tradition of interpretation in mind, in his first talk Buber asks the hearer/reader to consider what really happens in this tale. The rabbi tells his jailer, in effect, "You yourself are Adam, you are the one whom God asks: 'Where art thou?'" From the perspective of the philosophy of dialogue, the very meaning of our lives depends upon how we respond to this question. It is vital that you realize that God is calling for a personal response to a question addressed specifically to you alone, nothing else in Buber's talk matters.

Buber's initial interpretation of this story focuses on the rabbi's teaching style. Rather than using the text of Genesis as a chance to lecture the jailer, the rabbi uses it to directly challenge the chief for his irresponsible life. Pointing out that the rabbi's reply is given on a different plane from that on which the question is asked, Buber says:

> *Now, instead of explaining the passage and solving the seeming contradiction, the rabbi takes the text merely as a starting-point from where he proceeds to reproach the chief with his past life, his lack of seriousness, his thoughtlessness and irresponsibility.* (130)

In this interpretation of the story, the rabbi's response to the apparent contradiction of the all-knowing God's question is given on a different plane from that on which the question is asked. If, as Buber suggests, "in the beginning is relationship," our relationship with God begins with God's question to the first human: "Where are you in relation to me?" In the beginning of our becoming human, God asks us to enter into relationship with the ultimate source.

WHY THIS QUESTION?

Buber tells us that God's question is not asked to learn something that God doesn't already know but to produce an effect in the person that reaches his or her heart. One's answer to God's call cannot be restricted to any single interpretation or idea. Whatever answer one gives to the question is situation-determined and therefore ever new and ever unique. Like us, Adam hides to escape responsibility for his way of living. Adam, however, cannot hide from God and by attempting to do just that he is actually hiding from himself. God's question is designed to awaken you to your system of hideouts and to call you into relationship.

Follow Buber's reasoning as he examines the story more closely:

1. God's question is addressed to each person—to you yourself;
2. God's question is not designed to learn what God does not already know but to produce an effect in us, provided that the question reaches your heart;
3. To escape taking responsibility for his life, like Adam, we too construct a network of hideouts;

4. Although Adam (and the rest of us) cannot hide from the eye of God, in trying to do so Adam only manages to hide from himself;
5. God's question is designed to awaken Adam/us and to destroy our system of hideouts;
6. Everything depends on whether you face God's question, whether you take it to heart;
7. God's "still small voice" is easily drowned out and ignored;
8. As long as we ignore God's voice, no matter what success and power we achieve, our lives will not become a genuine path;
9. When Adam faces the Voice, and avows "I hid myself," this is the beginning of the human way;
10. There is a sterile kind of heart-searching that represents turning to God in hopelessness that leads only to despair.

FROM HIDING TO FACING

Buber says:

> *Adam hides himself to avoid rendering accounts, to escape responsibility for his way of living. Every* [person] *hides for this purpose, for every* [person] *is Adam and finds* [him or herself] *in Adam's situation. To escape responsibility for his life* [Adam] *turns existence into a system of hideouts. And in thus hiding again and again 'from the face of God,' he enmeshes himself more and more deeply in perversity.* (138)

If however you are attentive, a new situation arises, a new possibility—you recognize that you cannot escape the "voice" of God and at the same time there awakens in you a desire to come out of hiding.

What is the "still, small voice"? Is it the voice of God, our own voice, or the voice of a personal or communal conscience? The "still, small voice" that exists within and outside of each of us calls us to face our actions, our lives, and ourselves, all together. Buber says that every person, wishing to escape responsibility for his or her way of living, hides from this Voice. As long as this is continued, your life:

> *will not become a* way. *Whatever success and enjoyment* [you] *may achieve, whatever power* [you] *may attain and whatever deeds* [you] *may do,* [your] *life will remain way-less, so long as* [you do] *not face the Voice.* (134)

When Adam acknowledges that he hid himself, what is he doing? Why does his confession have the power to turn him from debasement and towards

God? It is his decisiveness, his honest self-exposure, that brings Adam out of hiding and that helps him to begin *unifying* himself. His turn in the direction of God puts him on the path towards himself, towards everyone, and towards God. This decisive turning with "holy intent" is what sets Adam, and all of us, on the way to genuine relationships.

ADAM'S/OUR CHALLENGE

For Buber, entering dialogue, whether with humans or with God, begins when we recognize that we, like Adam, are called to answer the question "Where are you?" whenever it is personally addressed to us. By answering it, we realize our uniquely human task of entering into genuine dialogue with the Eternal Thou. Like Adam, we hide from God to avoid rendering an account of our life and to escape responsibility for our way of living. Adam admits to the Voice that he was hiding because he was afraid. Yet God's question persists. Thus, Buber says:

> When the rabbi of Ger [near Warsaw], in expounding the Scriptures, came to the words which Jacob addresses to his servant: "When Esau my brother meets thee, and asks thee, saying, Whose art thou? And wither goest thou? And whose are these before thee?," he would say to his disciples: "Mark well how similar Esau's questions are to the saying of our sages: 'Consider three things. Know whence you came, wither you are going, and to whom you will have to render accounts.' Be very careful, for great caution should be exercised by him who considers these three things: lest Esau ask in him. For Esau, too, may ask these questions and bring man into a state of gloom."(135–36)

Heart-searching is decisive only if it leads to the human way. It seeks to know (1) whence you came, (2) where you are going, and (3) to whom you will render accounts. In other words, heart-searching is neither only intellectual nor primarily emotional. It becomes decisive only when the whole person, in body, mind, and spirit is prompted to turn and listen attentively for directions along his or her path in life. Buber continually distinguishes this from a second type of heart-searching that is sterile and that only partially addresses the individual. This ineffective and even self-destructive kind of heart-searching is intellectual, introspective, and self-analytical. Heart-searching is sterile when it comes from a spirit of hopelessness, from the sense that there is no way out from where you are. By contrast, genuine "Heart-Searching" means listening to the address of the signs that speak to your life even to those repressed forces that may contain the residue of our inmost passion.

THE QUESTION ITSELF

That God's first words to Adam/us ask a question is perfectly relational, not that God doesn't already know the answer, but that God wants to prompt us to make our most personal response. Discovering where we are begins when we respond honestly to this question. Paradoxically, God's question *places* us by temporarily *displacing* us from our comfort zones, the habitual, or conditional places that we occupy. God's question rubs up against us in ways that will not allow us to ignore it. It grips us; it stirs us up; it jostles us more than we can know on our own. Because it is a question that encourages, inspires, demands our most honest answer, our response both locates us and simultaneously hints at a direction of movement.

To realize how profound this question is, think for a minute from God's perspective. One may ask, "Can we really think from God's perspective?" It is, of course, impossible to know God's mind, yet it is worthwhile to try. That is, to fully respond to this question, it seems essential to imagine ourselves from God's point of view so as not to be trapped in private views and understandings. By imagining the impossible possibility of God's point of view, one may catch a glimpse of something that demands response with one's whole being. Such imagining is only possible with God's assistance, with much study, meditation, and direct prayer. Imagining God's perspective, although finally impossible, nevertheless draws us closer to God as the One who enters our domain intimately and immediately.

A blazingly clear exemplification of God's penetrating my autobiography occurred when, while still revising this manuscript, I had a conversation with Doug, a physicist and martial artist friend. He had just started reading Buber's *The Way of Man.* When I asked him "What has stood out for you so far in your reading?" he responded: "I'm fascinated with the fact that God began His-Her communication with Adam with this question. How profound," Doug said, his face lighting up. "It's perfect that God opens up a relationship with Adam precisely in the only way that God could." Doug's remark, given its timing, the high energy of its delivery, and the deep resonance that it struck in me brought me again to God's doorstep.

Think about it. How can God get into relationship with humans who know nothing of God in the first place? Remember, Adam/we are initially unknowing. Is there any better way for God to come into our lives other than by entering into our situation by asking a question? But why a question? Because thereby God shows immeasurable trust in Adam/us by being interested in his/our unique response. The entire dialogical relationship between God and Adam is only possible if it develops in mutual trust. Otherwise, it will pass away.

Even more important than the specifics of the question is that God asks it. This is how God establishes unconditional trust. What is the one thing necessary, after all, for a relationship to become genuine? Trust—trust that the other is making you present in this moment, that the other is really interested in what you say (even when disagreeing with it), and wants to continue being your dialogical partner. In this encounter, God, who is the "*mysterium tremendom*," the unimaginable Other, because of unconditional love becomes as "absolute Person" who is glimpsed in every genuine interaction. God's question comes to us in many forms through many different voices, expressed through people with whom we have genuine interaction. God's speech penetrates into and reveals itself in signs and insights, words and phrases and, like water, seeks the deepest level within our minds/hearts/souls. It is then our responsibility to be attentive (in reflection, in meditative thinking, in prayer) to these key moments in our lives.

LIVING THE QUESTION

How does this question affect your connection to God? Do you recognize resistance in yourself when you consider it? Or can you imagine how it could draw you into a deeper relationship with God? Not only is God's question addressed to Adam, to Abraham, to Jesus, not only is it likewise addressed to everyone and specifically to you, but God asks it again and again throughout your lifetime. But why make such a point of this? Because just as God's holy presence is revealed in ever-renewed ways, your response to it changes, matures, and grows as your circumstances and spiritual energy change.

The question "Where are you?" is categorically different from the question "Where am I?" that I ask myself. When I ask myself this question, I may have a large range of meanings in mind. I might be referring to a place or location, I might mean that I wish to encounter someone who can answer the central problem of my life, or I might simply be having an identity crisis. Whatever I mean when I ask myself where I am, I only enter into relation with myself. When the question comes from God, however, I am immediately drawn out of myself into an intimate relationship. God's question is existential, one that addresses both your heart and your mind, your feelings and your imaginings. As D. T. Suzuki put it, "the question is answered only when it is identified with the questioner."[1]

Buber says that the question "Where are you?" is designed to deconstruct your system of hideouts. Therefore, it is not necessarily a question that needs an immediate answer. Instead, it creates an opening through which to look out at life from a new vantage. In his *Letters to a Young Poet*, Rainer Maria Rilke writes:

> I want to beg you, as much as I can, . . . to be patient toward all that is unsolved in your heart and to try to love the questions themselves like locked rooms and like books that are written in a very foreign tongue. Do not now seek the answers, which cannot be given you because you would not be able to live them. And the point is, to live everything. Live the questions now. Perhaps you will then gradually, without noticing it, live along some distant day into the answer.[2]

Perhaps you do not need to come up with an immediate answer to God's question. Perhaps you can, instead, step inside the question and engage it at different times and in different situations. The question then becomes like a *mantra* which, when repeated, takes you more deeply into your relationship with God. It is *God*, after all, who asks you the question in the first place and who hopes for your unreserved honesty. Because your relationship to God is always changing, the more often you are addressed by the question, the better off you are in your spiritual growth.

As the contemporary Hasid Elie Wiesel has remarked, "A rebbe is someone who shares his questions with you. But then, if they are articulated with enough sincerity, the questions become answers, or at least they become a beginning of an answer."[3] For Elie Wiesel, what makes a rabbi's question worthwhile is the fact that it transfigures itself into an answer. Maurice Friedman adds that "No one can simply hand over the answers to us, but if we really hear the questions, take them into the depths of our souls, and make them our own, then our own answer may begin to take shape as a direction in which to move, a path to follow."[4]

How does this idea of living within the space opened up by an unanswered question strike you? Can you imagine what this might be like to live within the clearing, within the opening that God's question creates? What insights might arise, what breakthroughs might occur? As powerfully evocative and humbling as God's question is in the moment that you are addressed by it, its full impact does not cease after you make your initial response. The question continues to reverberate in our lives, often in surprising ways. One morning, for instance, I was talking to a realtor friend whose teenage twins had recently completed the first practice exercise listed at the end of this chapter—"If you perceived God addressing you personally with the question 'Where are you?' how would you respond? Do you agree or disagree with Buber? Why?"

"That question wasn't easy Kenny," he said.
"Not at all," I said. "So I appreciate your honesty."

"You have to be honest with Him," he said.

Then, as he prepared to leave he said, "What's next?"

Nothing came immediately to mind. Not wanting to speak too quickly, I paused and listened. Suddenly, I remembered that Buber's friend, Abraham Joshua Heschel once talked about considering ourselves from God's point of view. Then it became clear: "What's your question to God? What do you most want to ask God?" When he turned, smiling, to walk toward the pool, I called after him "Jim, there's one more thing. How do you imagine God responding?" Whose God?

Since the most important teaching of the first talk is that God calls us into relationship, it is important to understand who God was for Buber. It is understandable that many people are turned off by the word *God*. Is there another term more loaded down with misunderstanding than this one? For this reason, the venerable philosopher Paul Natorp once asked Buber

> How can you bring yourself to say *God* time after time? How can you expect that your readers will take the word in the sense in which you wish it to be taken? What you mean by the name of God is something above all human grasp and comprehension, but in speaking about it you have lowered it to human conceptualization.

Buber's response was empowered by the moment.

> "Yes," I said, "it is the most heavy-laden of all human words. None has become so soiled, so mutilated. Just for this reason I may not abandon it . . . Where might I find a word like it to describe the Highest! . . . And just for this reason is not the word *God* the word of appeal, the word which has become a *name*, consecrated in all human tongues for all time? . . . we cannot cleanse the word 'God' and we cannot make it whole; but, defiled and mutilated as it is, we can raise it from the ground and set it over an hour of great care."[5]

Buber acknowledged that the term God had been, and was still being used to justify horrible deeds, wars, and murder. Nevertheless, he refused to abandon the term. For Buber, the task was not to replace the word with a linguistic synonym, such as "Ground of Being" or "Ultimate Reality," but to deepen the power of its meaning in the context of living trust.

God is not an abstraction, a theological or metaphysical idea, or an object of religious belief. Rather, Buber points to the imageless God who is the Present One, who encounters humans in their daily activities. It can be said that God is, for Buber, the ever-unique, ever-particular, ever-personal, ever-loving, ever-dialogical "nameless meeter." "God," Buber once wrote, "cannot be expressed, only addressed." God, from this perspective is not a traditional, all-knowing, all-powerful, all-merciful entity who ultimately controls our lives from beginning to end. God refers to the Ultimate Source of life who simultaneously is wholly *other*, the *mysterium tremendum* beyond all knowing, wholly *same*, manifest through all sentient beings, and wholly *present* in this instant and in our midst as the Eternal Partner.

This realization is central. God for Buber becomes a dialogical partner who lovingly participates with us in acts of *ongoing* creation. Creation, you, and God are all partners in an immensely unimaginable and unpredictable cosmic dance. In it, God seeks to enter into a co-creative relationship with us such that life is not predetermined but always growing, always stumbling, always getting up, always creating. If this God asks you, "Where are you?" we might give a fundamentally different answer than one we would give to a wrathful, but mostly merciful, all-knowing God.

Our first task, then, is to forget everything that we think we know, what others have said, or what we have imagined God must be like. No matter how ingenious, no matter how descriptive, no matter how breathtaking a statement about God you hear, it cannot reveal the unutterable fullness of God's mystery. Who God really is will always outdistance our attempts to understand God. This is true because God's awesome mystery is simultaneously transcendent and immanent. God's immanence is always, according to Buber, ready to enter into a partnership with anyone who turns with his or her whole being towards the voice of the transcendent God. We might imagine turning to someone like the perfect listener: someone who not only hears every word, but also hears our thoughts, even those we are not yet aware of—one who completely understands what we mean by everything that we say and don't say and one who always responds honestly, compassionately, and justly.

DIVINE-HUMAN PARTNERSHIP

Buber speaks of our relationship to God as a partnership—the relation of a mutual need for the "other" that exists on both sides of the divine-human relationship. It is the *partnership* with the "eternal *Thou*" that makes possible every meaningful relation to the world. Since the "eternal *Thou*" is always becoming new, God can never be tied to dogmatic formulations or to specific rituals. And the mystery cannot be contained in a feeling. The "eternal *Thou*," in other words, is a living Presence who can never become an *It*. Nothing limits God. God is the ever-present partner throughout all of existence. As such, God is not to be found by leaving the world behind but by engaging it and sanctifying it with my whole being. Further, because each unique relationship leads to the Absolute, there is no need to seek God. There is nowhere that God cannot be found. Ironically, in fact, when we search for God we actually risk missing the very Person we're looking for.

For Buber:

Table 1.1.

GOD CANNOT BE . . .	INSTEAD, GOD . . .
Removed into a separate dimension	Penetrates our lives
Conceptualized in one's mind	Encounters us where we are
Dualized over and against the world	Relates to us dialogically
Absent from life	Is always uniquely present

God, for Buber, is not found by removing one's self from the world. Nor is God found by searching, because there is nowhere that God may not be found. God is not a being to be defined, or a proposition to be tested, or an interpretation to be believed or known. In place of offering an interpretation of who God is, Buber posits that the *presence* of God is glimpsed in interhuman relationships. According to Buber, we glimpse God not with our "mind's eye" but with our "being's eye." Reinforcing this point, Buber writes in *Eclipse of God* that "this glance of the being exists, wholly unillusory, yielding no images yet first making possible all images . . ."[6] That is, God cannot be spoken of in the third person, is not an idea, is not even a mystical experience.

GOD AS ABSOLUTE PERSON

The divine-human partnership to which God calls us cannot be understood independently of the relationship between one person and another. This is why Buber thought of God as the "absolute Person." As he wrote in his 1957 Postscript to *I and Thou*:[7]

> *The description of God as Person is indispensable for everyone who like myself means by "God" not a principle . . . and like myself means by "God" not an idea . . . but who rather means by "God," as I do, him who—whatever else he may be—enters into a direct relation with us men in creative, revealing and redeeming acts, and thus makes it possible for us to enter into a direct relation with him . . . As a Person God gives personal life, he makes us as persons become capable of meeting with him and with one another. But no limitation can come upon him as the absolute Person, either from us or from our relations with one another; in fact we can dedicate to him not merely our persons but also our relations to one another.*[8]

For Buber, God is the nearest One, the always ready, the supreme partner in dialogue.

How do you experience your connectedness to God? How and where does God directly address you? Can you think of ways to make this occur in your own life? Especially, Buber would highlight Hasidism's realization that God speaks to us through "the things and beings that He sends [us] in life" which we then answer through our "action in relation to just these things and beings."[9] Because engaging with God happens in this exact moment, it is *this* moment, Buber affirms, that must again and again be renewed by our full presence.

God addresses us, for Buber, by standing directly, nearly, and lastingly with us as the eternal partner who is always ready to become dialogically present. We might ask, though, what type of mutuality can exist between human beings and God. In Buber's words:

> *God's speech to men penetrates what happens in the life of each one of us, and all that happens in the world around us, biographical and historical, and makes it for you and me into instruction, message, demand. Happening upon happening, situation upon situation, are enabled and empowered by the personal speech of God to demand of the human person that he take his stand and make his decision. Often enough we think there is nothing to hear, but long before we have ourselves put wax in our ears. The existence of mutuality between God and man cannot be proved, just as God's existence cannot be proved.*[10]

God's speaking penetrates through every genuine interhuman relationship, especially when the words of others stand out as "instruction, message, demand." By turning to God with unreserved spontaneity, I bring all other relationships before God, to be transformed in God's presence. Our conversations with God and God's conversation with us happens in event-upon-event, happening-upon-happening. The personal address of God, through others, enables us to take a stand, to make decisions, and to continue in the direction of dialogue.

Even though God enters into our daily lives as absolute Person, God is always new in every situation, always uniquely manifested to each person. This is why we speak of "the God of Abraham, the God of Isaac, and the God of Jacob" rather than the "God of Abraham, Isaac, and Jacob." Each of these patriarchs of the Bible had his own unique relationship with God. Buber then suggests something that has become a powerful insight for me, one that continues to inspire and direct my spiritual journeying. Since God is fundamentally relational, according to Buber, God needs us to need God. That is, God continually creates me as a creative person. I am therefore responsible for becoming co-creative with God and others in the world in as many ways as possible.

BUBER LIFE ANECDOTE

In May of 1914, before the outbreak of the First World War, Buber received a visit from an old friend of his, Reverend Hechler, whom he had not seen for a long time. They spoke amicably for several hours. When they had reached the time for Hechler to leave, he asked Buber if he believed in God. Buber had a difficult time forming a reply since he did not reflect on God as a thing to be believed in. Buber reassured the retired reverend as best he could that he need have no concern about Buber's soul in this matter. Only later, on reflection, did he come to formulate a response:

> *If to believe in God means to be able to speak about him in the third person, then I certainly do not believe in God, or at least I do not know whether I may say that I believe in God. For I know well that if I speak of him in the third person, when that again and again happens, and it cannot at all be otherwise than that again and again happens, then my tongue is so quickly lamed that one cannot at all call that a speaking.*[11]

When Buber mentions that he does not *believe* in God, he means that he does not believe in the fictive God who is conditioned by his own perceptions and projections. That is, "[i]f to believe in God means to be able to talk about him in the third person," Buber would rather not speak of God at all. God was not the impersonal Godhead in the soul of the solitary mystic or the abstract God of the theologians. But, if "to believe in him means to be able to talk to him, then I believe in God." Buber's emphasis always remains on the *presentness* of God.

Each relational event with a particular other (whether a person, a place, or a thing), when genuine, affords a glimpse into a dialogical relationship with God. Rather than searching for God, therefore, Buber speaks of "a finding without seeking, a discovering of that which is most primal." This primal relationship—the fulfillment of each particular relationship—is present from the start. God is always new, "a moment's God" and "can only be addressed but not expressed."[12]

If you regard the essential element of your relation to God as an experience or feeling, like the overwhelming feeling of absolute certainty that occurs in your soul, it becomes easy to get sidetracked. Feelings are fleeting and partial. Every feeling is conditioned and defined by its opposite (e.g., love-hate, pleasure-pain). No matter how essential feelings may be, they only accompany, and need not control, the soul. Feelings are too easily suppressed, projected, or exaggerated. To overemphasize feelings is to misconstrue the complete character of the relationship that can only occur between persons and never, like an emotion, within an individual.

Since the extended lines of all genuine relationships intersect in the presence of God, it is relationship with each particular person that becomes the way to God. Buber writes:

> The [other] *meets me through grace—it is not found by seeking . . . The* [other] *meets me. But I step into direct relation with it. Hence the relation means being chosen and choosing, suffering and action in one; just as any action of the whole being, which means the suspension of all partial actions and consequently of all sensations of actions grounded only in their particular limitation, is bound to resemble suffering.*[13]

Genuine relationship embodies directness and wholeness, the will's intention to enter relationship, and the en-spiriting energy of grace. However, since genuine dialogue can only happen when one chooses to enter into relationship and *is chosen* by one who chooses to enter into relationship with you, dialogical wholeness involves both action and non-action. It cannot be forced into being.

CLOSING TALE

Buber frames each of his talks between two Hasidic tales, one at the beginning of his talk that sets the theme and another at the end that both develops the first tale and exemplifies its enactment. The first tale sets the topic in motion and the concluding tale develops and deepens it. The closing tale is told without much interpretation, which leaves us as readers free to engage it from our own places of understanding and presents us with the opportunity to express our own stand. In addition to expanding and clarifying what he has just said, Buber's selection of concluding tales also points ahead to what he will say in other talks. Placing the two tales in each talk side-by-side and comparing their insights provides us with a clearer understanding of Buber's intended meaning.

Highlighting the importance of heart-searching—searching for the human way—Buber selected a closing tale for his first talk that contrasts genuine heart-searching with sterile heart-searching:

> There is a demonic question, a spurious question, which apes God's question, the question of Truth. Its characteristic is that it does not stop at: "Where art thou?" but continues: "From where you have got to, there is no way out." This is the wrong kind of heart-searching, which does not prompt [you] to turn and put [you] on the way, but, by representing turning as hopeless, drives [you] to a point where it appears to have become entirely impossible and [you] can go on living only by demonic pride, the pride of perversity. (135–36)

This question is demonic because it presents the life of dialogue as hope-less. Here, the state of gloom into which our answers to life's most pressing spiritual question may bring us is the result of sterile heart-searching. It leads to nothing but self-torture, despair and still deeper enmeshment. For Buber, heart-searching becomes sterile when it leads us to the sense that there is no way out of our situation.

These final words bear close attention. Heart-searching completely mis-leads the spiritual seeker when it presents "turning as hopeless." When I say "I'll never find God," or "I'll never escape my situation," or "It's hopeless for me," inevitably I remain stuck. Sterile heart-searching undermines the one thing we absolutely need to offer a genuine response to God's question—the ability to turn with our whole being to God. For Buber, "turning" toward dialogue means turning away from self-centeredness and toward God as the source of life. So important is the practice of turning that Buber will return to it in his fifth talk.

So here it is—one thing is necessary (actually two things) to be able to make a genuine response to God's question. First, you must be willing to come out from hiding, from withdrawing, from not being fully attentive or fully present in this moment. That's first. Then, and only then, can you turn with your whole being to the question and simultaneously to the Eternal questioner. By facing up to our enmeshing hideouts, by facing the Voice, we/you can say whole-heartedly to the Ultimate dialogical partner: "Here I am!"

PRACTICE EXERCISES

At the conclusion of each chapter, you will have an opportunity to consider and engage three types of questions: (1) questions specifically addressing the chapter you have just read; (2) comparative questions relating to similar issues developed in the other talks; and (3) feedback questions designed to encourage you to enter into dialogue with others.

I. Chapter-Specific Questions

(Designed to bring greater clarity to Buber's central insights.)

1. If you perceived God addressing you personally with the question "Where are you?," how would you respond? Buber says that everything depends on how you answer God's call to Adam. Do you agree or disagree with Buber? Why?

2. How and where do you hide from God? Why? How and where do you hide from yourself?

3. In light of God's question to Adam, ask yourself a question put forth by the ancient Rabbis: How far along are you in your life? What have you accomplished? What is yet to be accomplished?

4. Buber says that sterile heart-searching does not prompt us to turn toward God, or toward others, and only makes it more difficult to answer God's question. Do you agree with this assessment? How might turning toward others better enable you to address God?

II. Comparative Questions

(Designed to deepen your dialogue with Buber's spiritual practices.)

1. Now and then a question addresses you with urgency yet it does not need an immediate answer. Consider an urgent question addressed to your life that would be helpful to live with without having a clear answer. Are you willing to live within this question and allow its echoes, its implications, its edges to affect the way you relate to the world? What happens to that question when you bring it, unanswered, into your dialogue with the world? When is the time right to return to the question and allow an answer to form itself for you?

2. Imagine yourself in a conversation with Buber about one of the questions that most challenges you or which, in your life, has caught you most by surprise. What do you think Buber would say? In response, what would you say to Buber?

3. What practice could you initiate, or intensify, in your life that would help you to embody the spirit of genuine dialogue? What is the first thing you would do? Then what?

4. With whom do you most identify in Buber's opening story: the jailer or the rebbe? How would you have acted either similarly or differently from the jailer?

III. Feedback Questions

(Designed to help you achieve life-integrations in meaningful dialogue with others.)

1. Select a question from the Chapter-Specific and Comparative Questions above. After engaging that question in dialogue with another person, what new insights and understandings emerged from the conversation?

2. Of the various responses you have made in your Journal, which one is of the greatest value to you where you are standing in life right now? How might you integrate your response into your daily life?
3. Create a dialogue script with Buber in which you ask a heartfelt question and then listen to hear Buber's response as if it was aimed uniquely at you. Before writing down "Buber's" answer, listen quietly to allow what Buber might say to form itself in your mind. Later, you may wish to share your dialogue script with someone.

Try to notice how your most pressing life-question and the way you have been answering it charges your dialogical relationships with others. What did you come to realize as a result of these dialogues? Record what you notice as you reflect on your meetings with others at the end of a day.

Chapter 2

Your Particular Way

"Our task is precisely to get in touch, by hallowing our relationship with what manifests itself in [the things and beings that we meet on our way], *as beauty, pleasure, enjoyment."* (143)

SUMMARY OF BUBER'S SECOND TALK

Buber begins the second talk, "The Particular Way," with the story of Rabbi Baer asking his teacher to show him a general way to serve God. This sets the tone for Buber's saying that there is no single way to serve God, that each person has a unique relationship to God, and that one's path toward God reflects one's uniqueness. At the same time, God is uniquely available to each person in a way most consonant with that person's abilities and potential. Whatever activity stirs your inmost desire expresses your unique path. The great spiritual teachings of history are but examples of what can be done. No single tradition or ritual should prevent you from finding the best pathway for yourself. Just so, the rabbi said, "Each of us in our own way shall devise something new in the light of teachings and of service, and do what has not yet been done." In Buber's telling of this Hasidic teaching, even inanimate nature carries within it the divine spark. For this reason, Buber affirms that the act of *hallowing* (making holy; sanctifying) your particular path is central to the human way. Our task is to hallow the world, especially our relationships with and in it with our whole being. This act leads to letting God in to our lives. Indeed, whatever you do may become a way to God provided you do it with your whole being. Essentially, to properly serve God, every person's unique task is precisely to get in touch with life by hallowing (sanctifying

21

everyday things and moments) your relationships with others and with God in your own way and with your whole being.

OPENING HASIDIC TALE

Buber begins his second talk by relating the tale of a rabbi who asked his teacher to show him a way to serve God.

Rabbi Baer of Radoshitz once said to his teacher, the 'Seer' of Lublin: 'Show me one general way to the service of God.'

The zaddik replied: 'It is impossible to tell men what way they should take. For one way to serve God is through learning, another through prayer, another through fasting, and still another through eating. Everyone should carefully observe what way his heart draws him to, and then choose this way with all his strength.' (138)

KEY TEACHINGS AND PRACTICES

Given the multiple ways in which one can serve God—by learning, prayer, fasting, or ritual eating—Buber suggests that you should observe carefully what draws your heart and choose this particular way with all your strength. Here, we come to a key moment in Buber's presentation: serving God finally is not a function of *what* specific things we elect to do (we can serve God with anything that we do) but *how* we do them. We serve God when, according to Buber, we serve others with our whole being, spontaneously, and without private agenda. This human wholeness not only marks all authentic activity, its action brings us into God's immediate and intimate presence.[1] Buber's interpretation of this second Hasidic tale refers us to concrete examples of genuine service and holy deeds found in the Jewish tradition. Drawing on examples of genuine service from the Jewish tradition, Buber suggests that, though we might revere them and learn from them, we should never attempt to imitate them. In the light of tradition, we must each find our own way, that is, it is the task of every person to find his or her own unique potential, to say "yes" or "no" to each possibility with conviction. To solidify this point, Buber interweaves three brief stories into his talk:

> The maggid [preacher] of Zlotchov [a town in Eastern Galicia] was asked by a Hasid: 'We are told: "Everyone in Israel is duty bound to say: When will my work approach the works of my fathers, Abraham, Isaac, and Jacob?" How are we to understand this? How could we ever venture to think that we could do

what our fathers did?' The rabbi expounded: 'Just as our fathers founded new ways of serving, each a new service according to his character: one the service of love, the other that of stern justice, the third that of beauty, so each one of us in his own way shall devise something new in the light of teachings and of service, and do what has not yet been done.' (139)

Each person in his or her own way represents something new, something uniquely original. Each person's foremost task, therefore, is not to repeat something that has already been done and recorded in books, but to actualize his or her "unique, unprecedented and never-recurring potentialities." This is why Rabbi Bunam teaches that rather than becoming like Abraham, it is important to become like ourselves:

The wise Rabbi Bunam once said in old age, when he had already grown blind: 'I should not like to change places with our father Abraham! What good would it do God if Abraham became like blind Bunam, and blind Bunam became like Abraham? Rather than have this happen, I think I shall try to become a little more myself.' (140)

In the same spirit, Rabbi Zusya said, a short while before his death, "In the world to come I shall not be asked: 'Why were you not Moses?' I shall be asked: "Why were you not Zusya?'" (140).

How do you access your individuality? How do you experience your connectedness to who you are? In response to what Zusya says, Maurice Friedman suggests that "We are called to become what we in our created uniqueness can become—not just to fulfill our social duty or realize our talent or potentialities, but to become the unique person we are called to be. This is not an already existing uniqueness that we can fulfill through 'self-expression' or 'self-realization.' We have to realize our uniqueness in response to the world. A part of this response, for Zusya, was the fact that Moses was there for him—not as a model to imitate but as an image of the human that arose in dialogue, a 'touchstone of reality' that entered into his own becoming."[2] That is, every person is called upon to fulfill her or his own unprecedented, never-recurring particularity.

The reason there is no general way to serve God is because of the uniqueness of the divine-human relationship. First, you, like everyone, are unique, never having been before, and never to be again. Second, God's presence is always new, original, and unpredictable. Third, your relationship to God is utterly new in every moment. Unlike anyone else's relationship to God, it is specific to your life, to your circumstances, to how far along the spiritual path you have traveled. For this reason, it makes sense to speak of the God of Abraham, the God of Isaac, the God of Jacob, the God of the prophets, the God of Jesus, your God, not as different Gods, but as different ways of relating to the holy One.

Each person has unique access to God's all-inclusiveness and infinite multiplicity. The Baal-Shem-Tov (the master of the name of God and the founder of Hasidism, Rabbi Israel ben Eliezer, 1700–1760) taught that every person should act and believe according to his or her life stand. If you follow another person's path, you will actualize neither your own path nor the other person's. Therefore, in the Hasidic tradition, we should behave according to the knowledge we have of our own selves. Doing this requires knowing your "essential quality and inclination," your "strongest feeling," the central wish of your inmost being.

ACCESSING GOD

Everyone has access to God, but each person has access to God in a different way. Because God is all-inclusive, there is an infinite number of paths that lead to God. When some Hasidim came to the Seer of Lublin and expressed surprise that his practices differed from those of their late master, the Seer exclaimed: "What sort of God would that be who has only one way in which he can be served!" God can be reached in multiple ways exactly because each person starts from his or her particular place determined by his or her particular nature. God does not say "This way leads to me and that does not," but says "Whatever you do may be a way to me, provided you do it in such a manner that it leads you to me." Trying to imitate someone else's service is a sure way to wander from the path of genuine dialogue:

> *The Baal-Shem said 'every man should behave according to his "rung." If he does not, if he seizes the "rung" of a fellow-man and abandons his own, he will actualize neither the one nor the other.' Thus the way by which a man can reach God is revealed to him only through the knowledge of his own being, the knowledge of his essential quality and inclination. 'Everyone has in him something precious that is in no one else.' (142)*

This precious something is revealed to you as your "strongest feeling," your "central wish," that which stirs your inmost being.

But how does one decide the best way to serve God? Indeed, how do you come to make any important decision? One popular way is to make a list of pros and cons about a given situation. This can sometimes be useful for people who need to frame a decision in terms of risks and benefits, who need to understand underlying psychological, social, and emotional components behind the decision they must make, and who need a way to methodically sort their options. For Buber, on the other hand, personal decisions are initiated and shaped dialogically. That is, for Buber, it is crucial to bring one's thought processes into engagement with others in order to hear how others respond to your ideas. It is in that process of give and take, of asking the right questions and listening carefully to the responses, that decision-making takes place.

At this point in his talk, Buber introduces a surprising possibility, the possibility of serving God with the "evil urge" of self-serving desire. Powerful desires that tempt us away from our path and toward self-satisfaction can be of potential benefit, provided that one is able to redirect one's passions for casual pleasures toward meeting essential life-goals. In order to find our way, Buber says, this impulse should "be diverted from the casual to the essential, and from the relative to the absolute." The "urge" must not be treated with "casual immediacy." It must become essential and absolute, not fleeting or necessitating instant gratification. Once self-serving desire makes the transition from the casual to the essential, it is no longer an "urge," but a hallowing of our relationships:

> A zaddik once said: 'at the end of Ecclesiastes we read: "at the end of the matter, the whole is heard: Fear God." Whatever matter you follow to its end, there, at the end, you will hear one thing: "Fear God," and this one thing is the whole. There is no thing in the world which does not point a way to the fear [awe] of God and to the service of God. Everything is commandment.' (142)

You may recall my brief conversation with physicist/martial artist Doug in the first chapter. He had just started reading Buber's *The Way of Man* and was deeply impressed that Buber would begin it with God's first words to Adam. "This question," Doug said, "much better than any I can imagine, levels the field between us and God. It indicates to me that God really wants to hear our free response. What an expression of trust on God's side," he affirmed.

A few days later, when I met him at the Health Club, I asked "Have you read any further."

"Yes," he responded. "I finished another chapter."

"And . . ." I said, eagerly, hoping that he would have a question.

"Why does Buber speak about the need to *fear* God?"

"Ah, no," I said, "*fear* is not the best translation here. It should read *awe*— the awe of God in the sense of radical amazement. How else can we respond to God's mysterious presence everywhere at once? How else can we react to the fact that all situations are holy?"

Doug then said something that indicated the maturity of his understanding of Buber's intention. "I thought that it must be a mistranslation because *fear* is the opposite of what Buber intends—namely, genuine relationship. Fear of the other would only hinder that." "Precisely," I said. "For Buber, it is necessary that we are in awe of God as the infinite source of life. In serving God, however, we do not turn from whom or what we meet along our way. Just the opposite. Our task is to hallow everything and everyone with whom we come in contact."

For some, Buber adds, fasting, asceticism, and mystical detachment may be a necessary starting-point to the deepest heart-searching, but we only come to know God by reverting to the world again. Any act, if hallowed by your intention, leads to God.

IN YOUR OWN WAY

Two interrelated motifs run through Buber's second talk: (1) that of finding your own way and (2) that of hallowing the everyday. Buber begins his commentary by speaking about our relationship to tradition, "to such general service as was performed by others before us." Each of us stands on the (intellectual, emotional, and spiritual) shoulders of genuine teachers whose words and actions remain for us lights that guide our journey. However, Buber adds, we should not try to imitate tradition:

> We are to revere it and learn from it, but we are not to imitate it. The great and holy deeds done by others are example for us, since they show, in a concrete manner, what greatness and holiness is, but they are not models which we should copy. However small our achievements may be in comparison with those of our forefathers, they have their real value in that we bring them about in our own way and by our own efforts. (138–39)

The last nine words in this passage—"in our own way and by our own efforts"—comprise the atmosphere of this talk and shape what Buber says following them. Buber insisted that no one had the right to prescribe the exact way to serve God for another person. Only you can discover the right way for you to be of service.

Alan Watts, one of the foremost Western interpreters of Eastern thought to Americans of the twentieth century, provides one good example of finding your own way. Born in England, Watts moved to California after first becoming an Episcopalian minister, a professor, and a graduate-school dean. In California, and throughout the United States, he lectured on Asian spirituality and mysticism, which he wrote about in books like *The Way of Zen, The Wisdom of Insecurity,* and *The Book: On the Taboo Against Knowing Who You Are.* In his autobiography—*In My Own Way*—he writes:

So I have always done things in my own way, which is at once the way that comes naturally, that is honest, sincere, genuine, and unforced; but also perverse, although you must remember that this word means *per* (though) *verse* (poetry), out-of-the-way and wayward, which is surely towards the way, and that to be queer—to "follow your own weird"—is wholeheartedly to accept your own *karma,* or fate, or destiny, and thus to be odd in the service of God, "whose service," as the Anglican Book of Common Prayer declares, "is perfect freedom."[3]

In Buber's words, it is our foremost task, our own particular duty, to "devise something new in the light of teachings and of service, and do what has not yet been done." Everyone has access to God's all-inclusiveness and to the multiplicity of ways that lead to God. Each of us, starting from our particular place and *being* in our own particular manner, is able to reach God. "God does not say: 'This way leads to me and that does not,' but he says: 'Whatever you do may be a way to me, provided you do it in such a manner that it leads you to me.'"

NOT WITHOUT TRADITION

All of this acting in your own way, however, if it is to be finally meaningful, happens in light of tradition. A rigorous approach to tradition can avoid mindless conformity on the one hand yet help being swept up in the tempo of the moment on the other. A rigorous tradition provides believers with a map of reality forged by the accumulated wisdom of centuries of co-believers. Such maps allow believers to examine the world intellectually, emotionally, and spiritually in order to delve into the mysteries of the universe. Of course, selecting the traditions that really addresses you at the core of your being is also a function of your own unique way of living. But what, after all, is "tradition"?

Far more than the teachings, beliefs, or practices of a single religion, sacred tradition stretches across many religious faiths, both eastern and western, and is embodied in and expressed through sacred texts. I agree completely with Max Müller, collector and translator of sacred texts of the ancient world, who compared scriptures to "grains of truth more precious to me than grains of gold. . . ."[4] As Müller remarks elsewhere, the world's religious texts have become "sacred heirlooms, sacred because they come from an unknown source from a distant age."[5] Whether its authority has been established by a holy person, by its use in rituals, or by the spiritual potency of its words, scripture is a sacred tradition's most authoritative voice.

In my more than forty years of study and practice within various traditions, especially Christian (first Baptist, then Catholic), Indic (especially Rinzai

Zen), and Hasidic, it has been impossible for me simply to accept each and every sacred text literally, or even symbolically and allegorically. Literal, symbolic, and allegorical understandings of scripture, while valuable along the way, remain one-sided and intellectually motivated. Instead, following Buber, it has become necessary for me to read and understand sacred texts through dialogue with them. This dialogue is really a three-part interaction, for between me and a sacred text lies the dimension of meaning that emerges from the dialogue itself. Real understanding of a sacred text, when it emerges from this dialogue, is ever-new and ever-renewing. Living in my own way in the light of tradition, accordingly, involves entering constantly into genuine dialogue with tradition. The anchoring influence of tradition, dialogically understood, keeps the "in my own way" but is not, for Buber, merely a license to do as I please.

BUBER'S RELATION TO TRADITION

What about Buber's own relation to tradition? Religious tradition, according to Buber, was a double-edged sword that "constitutes the noblest freedom for a generation that lives it meaningfully." Yet it can be "the most miserable slavery for the habitual inheritors who merely accept it tenaciously and complacently" (*On Judaism*, 11). Buber insisted that a person retains the responsibility of interpreting tradition from the place where one stands. Perhaps the most important thing Buber said in his discussions regarded his relationship to Judaism. Asked about the Jewish law, or *Halakhah*, Buber conceded that his position might be mistaken for antinomianism or lawlessness, and that it might be used by an irresponsible person to confirm him in his irresponsibility. But for the responsible person, Buber saw the personal as the only way. "In three hundred years there may be a new *Halakhah*," Buber said:

> But now this is just the way of the modern [person]. I am only against life becoming rigid. I want to warn [everyone] against anticipated objectification. Of course, objectification will come again and again, and when it does, the tradition can only be renewed through the personal way. On the personal way one may discover things that are not only true for oneself but for others. One cannot live without danger, without risk—the question is to choose between risks. [6]

In no sense did Buber proceed as a theologian who accepts what the tradition says simply because it is the tradition. He would only affirm what he could confirm out of his own personal testing and wrestling. "There are things in the Jewish tradition I cannot accept at all," Buber told us, "and things I hold true that are not expressed in Judaism. But what I hold essential has been expressed more in biblical Judaism than anywhere else—in the biblical dialogue between us and God. "In Hasidism," he continued, "this is developed in a communal life. I want to show that Judaism can be lived. It is most important that the Jews today live Judaism."[7]

The following episode, therefore, is not at all surprising. Buber scholar and friend Maurice Friedman tells of Buber's advice to him in response to what Abraham Joshua Heschel had once suggested to Friedman. Heschel very much wanted Friedman to begin being an observant, practicing Jew. Friedman never felt fully at ease with the fact that he had not entered a specific spiritual practice. Dr. Heschel often questioned this from the standpoint of the need for community and prayer, the need to be filled with *kavana* but not to be set aside until *kavana* comes.

Friedman wrote to Buber requesting advice on the matter of observing Jewish ritual and law, as much to better understand Buber's views on the question as to work through his personal conflict about befriending these two men, immersing himself in the dialogical theory of Hasidic Judaism on the one hand and on the other in the views of one who saw observation of Jewish custom as imperative to practicing Judaism. Friedman told Buber:

> There is little to be hoped. Yet I am sometimes troubled by the absence of any set or extensive religious observance in my own life. This trouble comes from my previous period of mysticism when religious practice was a central part of life as well as from the insistence of Dr. Heschel that one can only understand Judaism by taking part in it, that *kavana* does not come by itself apart from daily prayer.

Buber however replied, characteristically, that he could not see a problem like this independently of his personal experience. Buber wrote:

> *How can I make this into a general rule about ritual being right or wrong and so on? I open my heart to the Law to such an extent that if I feel a commandment being addressed to me I feel myself bound to do it as far as I am addressed—for instance, I cannot live on Sabbath as on other days, my spiritual and physical attitude is changed, but I have no impulse at all to observe the minutiae of the Halakha about what work is allowed and what not. In certain moments, some of them rather regular, some other just occurring, I am in need of prayer and then I pray, alone of course, and say what I want to say, sometimes without words at all, and sometimes a remembered verse helps me in an extraordinary situation; but there have been days when I felt myself compelled to enter into the prayer of a community, and so I did it. This is my way of life, and one may call it religious anarchy if he likes. . . . I cannot say anything but, put yourself in relation as you can and when you can, do your best to persevere in relation, and do not be afraid![8]*

YOUR RELATION TO TRADITION

How does Buber's point strike you? And why is it necessary for us to make such a point of this? It is important for me because spiritual life does not presuppose any one interpretation of tradition to be the correct one. Just as everything we know is our interpretation of what we know, so too it can never be "objectively" known for the knower is an integral part in the process. Yet if neither I nor anyone else can know the truth objectively, how should I proceed to search for an ever-deepening grasp of a teaching or practice? Simple. There must be room for ever-new interpretations. Throughout different historical epics, persons have found their own interpretations, the ones best suited to their time and place, to their context, to their needs.

The relationship between Hasidic tradition and the person you are at this moment is one of renewal—of bringing the teaching to life in the present. While we live within the always-existing tension between the past and the present, between tradition and who I am at this moment, it is necessary to listen deeply and respond dialogically to the sacred texts and to enter into dialogue with others about them. For this reason, as we recall, the Baal-Shem said:

> "We say: 'God of Abraham, God of Isaac, and God of Jacob,' and not: 'God of Abraham, Isaac, and Jacob,' for Isaac and Jacob did not base their work on the searching and service of Abraham; they themselves searched for the unity of the Maker and his service."[9]

In the Hasidic view, our relation to tradition rests, ironically, on not swallowing it whole but on continually entering into dialogue with it from where we each stand in the world.

I once dreamed for instance that I was in a private conversation with a Benedictine monk and priest, the author of several books including one on the Gospel of John, who had presided at my reception into the Church more than 30 years ago. With ever-deepening respect, over the years I had come to regard him as a spiritual mentor. In the dream, I was very concerned about something that Jesus is reported to have said. I asked him "Do you believe that Jesus actually said what he is reported to have said in the Gospels about founding the church on Peter's faith?" In response, he said, "You have to find your own way."[10]

He did not answer my question, as one might expect from a monastic and theologian (even a dreamed one!), in a way that would have engaged me at the level of biblical scholarship. Instead, like a Hasidic rabbi, he completely shifted our dialogue by responding to a deeper, unasked question. His answer recognized that I was really asking a much deeper question than what Jesus meant. I was inquiring into my relation to the whole tradition. And in his answer he pointed me to the utter significance of coming to discover the meaning of that relationship myself.

THE RIGHT WAY

Fittingly, in Buber's understanding of the Jewish Jesus, it should be noted, Jesus was a reformer, a Jew who did not accept everything as it was handed down from his forefathers and taught by the rabbis and Pharisees. Instead, Jesus expressed the central teachings of his tradition through his intimate, immediate, dialogical relation with God. This is nowhere more evident than in Jesus' prayer, the "Our Father," in which he taught an altogether new way of addressing God as "Abba," an intimate name for God as a confidant, as a friend, as a dialogical partner.

There are many ways to find one's unique path in the light of tradition. The point is to find that one way which is wholly yours and then to fulfill it in as many meetings, interactions, and life events as possible. For me, one right path is the Buddhist's eight-fold path in which one acts in the spirit of right understanding, right resolve, right speech, right acts, right livelihood, right effort, right mindfulness, and right concentration. This path is walked by Buddhists in order to break out of enslavement to desires, which are never satisfied and which only produce more desires. The common denominator in this list is the word "right," which means doing whatever you're doing in the "right" manner.

But what is the right way to do anything? For the practicing Christian, the right way would be surrendering wholeheartedly into prayer with God. For the practicing Buddhist, the right way is any way empty of self, empty of attachment to the doing. This means acting in a way that eliminates the distinction between me and the action I'm taking. It is as if, by acting, I am being acted upon.

Religious tradition, according to Buber, was a double-edged sword that "constitutes the noblest freedom for a generation that lives it meaningfully." Yet it can be "the most miserable slavery for the habitual inheritors who merely accept it tenaciously and complacently." (*On Judaism*, 11) Buber insisted that a person retains the responsibility of interpreting tradition from the place where one stands.

Once, for instance, in a December 31st conversation with Nick, who was raised in the Greek Orthodox tradition, I brought up my interest in Benedictine monasticism, especially because of monks like Thomas Merton and Brother David Steindel-Rast, who participate in interreligious dialogue. "Do you know Thomas Hopko," he asked.

"Yes," I replied, "I know that he is well respected in the Orthodox community and that he also participates in interreligious dialogue." In my mind I could see a book with his name on it but could not discern its title.

"Once," Nick said, "after he gave a talk to a Buddhist group, someone asked 'In Mahayana Buddhism, there is an axiomatic teaching that says: If you meet the Buddha on the road, kill him.' Is there any axiomatic statement in Christianity like this one?" Hopko replied, 'No. Yet I can imagine one like this: If you meet Christ on the road let him kill you.' Those present were amazed. No one had ever heard anything like that before."

Hopko's faith statement expanded the outer edges of Christian tradition. I thanked him for the New Year's gift of this episode, which challenged me to renew my own dialogue with Jesus and with what Christian tradition teaches about Jesus. Buber on the other hand would probably say that rather than killing or being killed by the other, it is necessary to enter into a genuine relationship with the other.

Once you discover how to put God first—in everything—how to always remember your partnership with God, how to be God-infused, God-influenced, whether in eating, or working, or praying, or studying; once you discover how to put God first you can do it in every situation.

HALLOWING

By hallowing (from the German verb *heiligen*, to make holy) the everyday, Buber means approaching life with a reverential attitude that helps us to open out to transcendence. Hallowing refers to a radical shift in your life-stance, in your attitude, that manifests a reverence for everything you encounter. Entering into holy interaction with the world, a person liberates the divine spark that is "imprisoned in the shells in which society, state, church, school, economy, public opinion and your own pride have imprisoned you. . . ." and awaiting release in all things and people. Buber wrote that our task in life is to prepare a dwelling place for God's grace, which wants to come into the world through us.[11]

> *Hallowing is an event which commences in the depths of a* [person], *there where choosing, deciding, beginning takes place. The* [person] *thus enters into the hallowing. But* [one] *can only do this if* [one] *begins just as* [a human being] *and presumes to no superhuman holiness.*[12]

What hallowing means is unique in each life situation, which is why Buber speaks of hallowing your relationship to whatever encounters you and making holy your actions. Everything wants to be hallowed, to be brought into holiness—eating and drinking, working and playing, reading and writing, listening and praying, everything. In his fifth talk, he will speak of hallowing your soul. Though the act of hallowing differs from situation to situation, its outcome is always similar—it leads to communion with the divine absolute. Hallowing is so important, Buber says, that by no means:

> can it be our true task, in the world into which we have been set, to turn away from the things and beings that we meet on our way and that attract our hearts; our task is precisely to get in touch, by hallowing our relationship with them, with what manifests itself in them as beauty, pleasure, enjoyment. Hasidism teaches that rejoicing in the world, if we hallow it with our whole being, leads to rejoicing in God . . . Any natural act, if hallowed, leads to God, and nature needs man for what no angel can perform on it, namely its hallowing. (143)

Buber uses the word hallowing six times in the last two paragraphs of this talk, suggesting its importance and centrality to the life of dialogue.

We can understand hallowing better if we see it as a sacrament. Writing about Buber's emphasis on sacramental existence, Maurice Friedman suggests that humans "have been placed in the world that we may raise the dust to the spirit. Our task, as long as we live, is to 'struggle with the extraneous and uplift and fit it into the divine Name.' All sacraments have at their core something natural taken from the course of life that becomes consecrated through the meeting of the human and the divine. But the heart of sacrament is that it does not level the sacrament down to a symbolic gesture or overly exalt it to 'an exuberantly heartfelt point.' Instead, it 'includes an elementary, life-claiming, and life-determining experience of the *other*, the otherness, as of something coming to meet one and acting toward one.' Therefore, sacramental existence is not merely celebrated or experienced. It seizes and claims the human being in the core of his wholeness and needs nothing less than his wholeness in order to endure. 'There is,' when we sacramentally hallow the everyday, 'no rung of human life on which we cannot find the holiness of God everywhere and at all times.'"[13]

HOLY INTENT

Does this teaching of hallowing reverberate in your own heart? And if so, how are you to implement it? Is it possible to hallow all life by yourself, without assistance? At its deepest, hallowing refers to opening out towards transcendence by responding to every day relationships with "holy intent." This requires attending to the presence of the mysterious divine spark in

whomever or whatever you encounter in the world. Not only is it imperative to intentionally put hallowing into your everyday practice—here, there,
and everywhere—but it is also necessary to hallow your intention itself. By
hallowing your intention to make all life holy, not only do you reinforce this
intention and make it more likely to be put into practice from your side, but
as well you invite God's participation with you in the process. When an act
is done, a prayer uttered, a choice made with genuine *kavana*, it is an act
of wholeness and thus genuine resolution. The practice of hallowing thus
becomes a joint venture so to speak. My separate "I" disappears into "We."
When I/you make all life sacred, We (I/you and God) make it so.

I once told a young, church-going father of two accomplished swimmers
about a series of classes that I was teaching on Dialogical Spirituality. Weeks
later, he asked me how the classes were going. "Scott," I said, "today's class
will be the final one!"

"Oh," he said, "I'm so glad to hear that. So what's today's class about?"

"Hallowing each event, each activity of our lives," I said. "It's about a radical shift in our attitude from self-centeredness, from entering each moment
thinking only about ourselves to entering each moment with a reverence for
the relationships that we are entering. It's about having this attitude as a frame
through which we walk towards whom or what we are about to encounter."

"It's unbelievable that you just said that," he said, "because I've been
struggling this week with my life; I've been constantly pulled out of the present and into the past or the future. And I've been wondering how I can stay in
the moment better. And that's it. Having that attitude of revering the moment
and letting it lead me into the next moment."

But why make such a point of this? That's easy to answer. Everything in
the world calls for hallowing, and our task is to practice hearing and responding to that call. As Buber wrote in his classic *I and Thou*, "*if you hallow this
life you meet the living God.*"[14] For Buber, the act of hallowing meant intentionally and unconditionally revering or respecting life. Hasidism emphasizes
rejoicing in the world, which we can accomplish if we "hallow it with our
whole being." Such hallowing leads to rejoicing in God.

BUBER LIFE ANECDOTE

One of the best exemplifications of the theme of Buber's second talk—
discovering your own way to serve God—is Buber's own relationship to
Hasidism. Buber's way to Hasidism began in his childhood, when he was
occasionally taken by his father to the village Sadagora, the seat of the Hasidic
zaddikim (the righteous, the proven). The Hasidic communities that once

upheld the "high faith" and "fervent devotion" of the zaddikim, Buber came to feel, no longer existed. Rather, he writes, present-day Hasids turn to the tales of the zaddikim as "the mediator through whose intercession they hope to attain the satisfaction of their needs." Even in these "degenerate Hasidim," though, there continued to glow the tales of the rebbes. As Buber relates his experiences:

> *The place of the rebbe, in its showy splendor, repelled me. The prayer house of the Hasidim with its enraptured worshipers seemed strange to me. But when I saw the rebbe striding through the rows of the waiting, I felt, "leader," and when I saw the Hasidim dance with the Torah, I felt "community." At the time there rose in me a presentiment of the fact that common reverence and common joy of soul are the foundations of genuine human community.*[15]

This early impression was followed by periods of doubt and confusion. Still, Buber professed Judaism without, as he said, really knowing it. What Buber sought was "immediate knowing, the eye-to-eye knowing of the people in its creative, primal hours."

Then, later in life, came his transformation. One day, on opening the testament of Rabbi Israel Baal-Shem, he writes:

> *the words flashed toward me, "He takes unto himself the quality of fervor. He arises from sleep with fervor, for he is hallowed and become another man and is worthy to create and is become like the Holy One, blessed be He, when He created His world." It was then that, overpowered in an instant, I experienced the Hasidic soul. The primally Jewish opened to me, flowering to newly conscious expression in the darkness of exile: man's being created in the image of God I grasped as deed, as becoming, as task. And this primally Jewish reality was a primal human reality, the content of human religiousness. Judaism as religiousness, as "piety," as Hasidut opened to me there. The image out of my childhood, the memory of the zaddik and his community, rose upward and illuminated me: I recognized the idea of the perfected man. At the same time I became aware of the summons to proclaim it to the world.*[16]

Still, throughout his life, Buber continued to question and doubt elements of his faith, writing that he himself was

> *truly no zaddik, no one assured in God, rather a man in danger before God, a man wrestling ever anew for God's light, ever anew engulfed in God's abysses. . . .*[17]

He confessed in his writings that

> *I have not been able to accept either the Bible or Hasidism as a whole; in one and in the other I had to and I have to distinguish between that which had*

*become evident to me out of my experience as truth and that which had not
become evident to me in this manner.*[18]

Buber, in other words, followed Hasidic teachings in his own way—never
swallowing them whole but reforming them according to his understanding,
situation, and spiritual practice.

In his study of Hasidism, as a consequence, Buber reformed the Hasidic
teachings, but not radically. He believed that continual reform was at the heart
of Hasidism itself, but Buber did not alter Hasidism's fundamental substance.
Rather, through the Hasidic tales and his dialogue with them, Buber found
his own particular, unique, idiosyncratic, for the first time way to serve God.
His relationship to the tradition was shaped, informed, and influenced by the
teachings and practices that grasped him. Yet he reshaped these teachings and
practices by the force of his own personality, training, and most significantly,
relationship with God.

Buber embraced but did not imitate Hasidic tradition. Instead, he embodied
a creative relation to it that focused closely on the teaching substance and
style of the Hasidic tales. Buber's path unfolded in the dialogue between the
scholar, the teacher, the writer, and the realized fulfillment of the tales. As
Buber once reflected, in Hasidic teaching he found

*the strongest witness for the primacy of the dialogical that is known to me.
Certainly this witness has been the divining-rod that has led me to water; but
the water itself could not have been anything other than the experience of faith
that fell to my share.*[19]

CLOSING TALE

Unlike the Hasidic tales that generate Buber's commentary at the beginning
of each talk, the closing tales are largely and intentionally left open to the
reader's dialogue with them. The closing tale of his second talk emphasizes
the act of hallowing the everyday:

*The biblical passage which says of Abraham and the three visiting angels:
'And he stood over them under the tree and they did eat' is interpreted by
Rabbi Zusya to the effect that man stands above the angels, because he knows
something unknown to them, namely, that eating may be hallowed by the eat-
ers intention. Through Abraham the angels, who were unaccustomed to eating,
participated in the intention by which he used to dedicate it to God. Any natural
act, if hallowed, leads to God, and nature needs man for what no angel can
perform on it, namely, its hallowing.* (144)

In this passage man stands above the angels because he knows something unknown to them, namely, that eating may be hallowed by the eater's intention. This tale re-emphasizes that hallowing, which leads to God, is a function of your holy intention as you find your own way. Hallowing any natural act—what you are doing right now, for instance—when performed with holy intent, opens the way toward genuine dialogue.

PRACTICE EXERCISES

I. Chapter-Specific Questions

(Designed to bring greater clarity to Buber's central insights.)

1. Name or describe a specific way in which you serve God. Does it differ from your other activities? If so, how?
2. Buber says that everyone should behave according to his or her "rung," or place in the world, which is revealed when you perceive your strongest feeling or central wish. How do you respond to this? Do you agree or disagree with Buber? Why?
3. How does Rabbi Zusya's remark that "any natural act, if hallowed, leads to God" strike you? Does it need to be qualified in any way? Is there any act in your life that has not led to God? Can you imagine it ever leading to God?
4. What prevents you from realizing and practicing your own unique task in life? How can you reverse this?

II. Comparative Questions

(Designed to deepen your dialogue with Buber's spiritual techniques.)

1. Now and then a question addresses you without needing an immediate answer. Select one important life question that might be helpful to live with without your having a clear answer to. Are you willing to live within the question, so to speak, and allow your dialogue with it to affect the way you relate to the world? What happens to that question when you bring it, unanswered, into your discourse? When is the time right to return to the question and allow an answer to form itself for you?
2. Imagine yourself in a conversation with Buber about one of these questions that most challenges you or which most surprises you. What do you think Buber would say? In response, what would you say to Buber?

3. Following Buber's interpretation of the Hasidic tradition in this presentation, what practice could you initiate or intensify in your life that would help you to hallow the every day? What is the first thing you would do? Then what?
4. What does the dynamic relation between rebbe and disciple in the opening tale indicate about the disciple's behavior? With whom do you most identify in this story? How would you have acted either similarly or differently than the disciple?

III. Feedback Questions

(Designed to help you achieve life-integrations in meaningful dialogue with others.)

1. Select a question from the Chapter-Specific and Comparative Questions above. After engaging that question in dialogue with another person, what new insights and understandings emerged from the conversation?
2. Of the various responses you have made in your Journal, which one is of the greatest value to you where you are standing in life right now? How might you integrate your response into your daily life?
3. Create a dialogue script with Buber in which you ask a heartfelt question and then listen to hear Buber's response as if it was aimed uniquely at you. Before writing down "Buber's" answer, listen quietly to allow what Buber might say to form itself in your mind. Later, you may wish to share your dialogue script with someone.
4. Try to notice how your most pressing life-question and the way you have been answering it charges your dialogical relationships with others. What did you come to realize as a result of these dialogues? Record what you notice as you reflect on your meetings with others at the end of a day.

Chapter 3

Resolution

"Any work that I do with a united soul reacts upon my soul, acts in the direction of new and greater unification, leads me, though by all sorts of detours, to a steadier unity than was the preceding one." (150)

SUMMARY OF BUBER'S THIRD TALK

Buber begins his third talk, "Resolution," telling of a Hasidic Jew who fasted from one Sabbath to the next, wavered, was tempted to take a drink, restrained himself, felt pride, and then noticed that his thirst subsided. When he entered his teacher's house, the rabbi chided him, describing his efforts as "patchwork." Buber explains that in his youth he felt that the rabbi acted harshly. Long afterward, Buber recognized that what the Hasid lacked was a "united soul." Before undertaking any unusual feat such as a week-long fast, a unified soul is necessary. But unification of the soul, in other words pulling yourself together, becoming "all of a piece," is never complete. It needs to happen again and again in every activity one engages in. For this reason, Buber says, "any work that I do with a united soul . . . acts in the direction of new and greater unification, leads me . . . to a steadier unity than was the preceding one." Therefore, there comes a point where a person can rely on his or her soul and will overcome contradictions "with effortless ease." Essentially, before undertaking any spiritual practice, it is necessary to be resolved to unify your soul, to straighten yourself out by refocusing on the goal and by remaining wholly open to whatever addresses you in partnership with the Divine Presence.

OPENING HASIDIC TALE

Buber begins his third talk by retelling a Hasidic tale about a conflicted student:

> A hasid of the Rabbi of Lublin once fasted from one Sabbath to the next. On
> Friday afternoon he began to suffer such cruel thirst that he thought he would
> die. He saw a well, went up to it, and prepared to drink. But instantly he real-
> ized that because of the one brief hour he had still to endure, he was about to
> destroy the work of the entire week. He did not drink and went away from the
> well. Then he was touched by a feeling of pride for having passed this difficult
> test. When he became aware of it, he said to himself, 'Better I go and drink than
> let my heart fall prey to pride.' He went back to the well, but just as he was
> going to bend down to draw water, he noticed that his thirst had disappeared.
> When the Sabbath had begun, he entered his teacher's house. 'Patchwork!' the
> rabbi called to him, as he crossed the threshold. (146)

KEY TEACHINGS AND TECHNIQUES

In this talk, the Hasid tests himself, and has good intentions in doing so, but he is not yet wholly unified, not fully resolved. He embarks upon his test, to fast for one week, and finds himself vacillating at the end, showing that he is still "fighting" against his physical self with his spiritual self. As a result, he cannot complete his test without becoming self-involved. When he becomes thirsty, and feels as if he is about to die, he decides to drink, but he stops himself at the last moment. He at first feels pride at his self-control, but then decides to drink in order to not commit the sin of pride. Finally, he no longer feels thirst. When he meets the rabbi, his zaddik refers to his spiritual development as "Patchwork" because the Hasid does not yet have a unified soul. As a result, he is not ready to commit to denying his physical self. He cannot complete work that is "all of a piece" until he finds that he himself is "all of a piece." His intense denial of the physical self leads to the inconsistency of the interior/spiritual self. It draws too much attention to physical *need*.

Buber's interpretation of the opening tale passes through at least three phases: his initial youthful encounter with it; his return to it long afterwards; and his return to it again with renewed scrutiny. In his youth, Buber was struck by the harsh way in which the Hasidic teacher treats his disciple. Later, when Buber was retelling the tale, he realized that the teacher, by allowing the disciple to practice fasting at least for a time, does so to raise the disciple's awareness to a higher level before criticizing his wavering.

When Buber subjected the story to renewed scrutiny, he came to understand the Rabbi's main teaching—the necessity of becoming unified before
undertaking one's work. In this tale, Buber says, "the disciple's first inhibi-
tion was due to the power of the body over the soul, a power which had still
to be broken." But why does the power of the body over the soul need to be
broken? If we deny our spiritual self, we are "hiding" from God *and* from
ourselves. If we deny our physical self, our bodies, we are doing the same.
The Hasid was conflicted. He realized that he could not deny his body any-
more. Yet he was committed to the task of caring for his soul.

WHAT IS THE SOUL?

In Maurice Friedman's paraphrasing of this tale, the "Seer of Lublin had a
disciple who fasted from Sabbath to Sabbath, which in the Jewish tradition
meant taking neither food nor water. An hour before the end of the week, the
disciple thought he would die if he did not take a drink of water. When he
reached into the well for a drink, he thought, 'a whole week's work wasted!'
This thought helped him overcome the temptation, but overcoming the
temptation made him feel pride. When he became aware of this, he decided
to make himself drink after all. Somehow he overcame this temptation too,
and finished the week without breaking his fast. When he crossed the Seer's
threshold, the Seer, as we have seen, came out to greet him not with congratu-
lations but with the word, 'patchwork!' In this 'cruel' way he taught him the
difference between a work done all of a piece and a 'spiritual achievement'
that is of no value because it is not done with the whole soul."[1]

But what is the soul? From Buber's perspective, there is a good deal of
misunderstanding about the soul, especially by those who reduce the soul to
an interior location or experience. Carl Jung, to mention just one example,
used to encourage his clients to write all of their dreams, visions, nightmares,
and inspirations in a beautifully bound notebook. Then, as he suggested to a
particular client,

> . . . when these things are in some precious book you can go to the book and
> turn over the pages & for you it will be your church—your cathedral—the silent
> places of your spirit where you will find renewal. If anyone tells you that it is
> morbid or neurotic and you listen to them—then you will lose your soul—for
> in that book is your soul.[2]

Buber, by contrast, speaks of the soul as the whole person (body/mind/spirit)
united in one's heart and in relation to the world. For Buber, the soul does

not exist just *in* a person, in the "I," but is expressed in the interactive realm *between* a person and what confronts her or him in the world. Buber attributes what he calls the madness of the present time to the fact that:

> *In place of the soul, which is a plane of relationship between* [person] *and world, an all-penetrating substance is created: all is transformed into soul. This fact is the true fall. Here first the fall takes place.*[3]

Unifying one's soul, therefore, for Buber, equals unifying your relationship to the world. This means an unreserved engagement with the world, a type of engagement in which you do not withhold yourself or leave any of yourself out.

Jung's view of the soul, if it is relational at all, is at best monological. That is, I have a relationship between myself and what I create, or envision, or intuit emerging from my own "unconscious." For Buber, by contrast, my soul is always arising in relation to the world:

> *"With all his soul.* [a person] *who decides with all his soul decided for God; for all wholeness is God's image, shining from within His own light. In that true, unifying decision in which dualism is abolished, the primal intent of the world is fulfilled, in eternal renewal.*[4]

Buber goes even further:

> *It is not the soul, but the whole of the world, which is meant to be redeemed in the redemption.* [Humans] *stand created, a whole body, ensouled by . . . relation to the created, enspirited by . . . relation to the Creator. It is to the whole* [person], *in this unity of body, soul, and spirit, that the Lord of Revelation comes and upon whom He lays His message.*[5]

BODY, MIND AND SPIRIT

In his youth, upon hearing the opening tale for the first time, the master's response seemed too harsh to Buber. "How could the Hasid be scolded for such an inner struggle? Is that not asking too much of a person?" Long afterwards, however, when Buber retold this tale, he realized that the zaddik was calling his disciple to "a higher rung." Buber realized that the zaddik's rebuff was aimed not at the disciple's fasting, which might lift his soul to a higher rung, but at the divided, complicated, and contradictory soul that caused his wavering. The opposite of "wavering" was to be "all of a piece," no longer a patchwork, but whole cloth. Upon deeper reflection, Buber realized that the disciple was being called—"by nature or grace"—to achieve a "unified soul, a soul all of a piece" in whatever he did. The person who "wavers" is called to "pull himself together," to "reconcentrate upon the goal," and even to sacrifice the goal to become whole.

In light of these reflections, Buber subjected the story to further scrutiny. How can the soul that is conflicted or divided be unified? Buber asked himself. He concluded that:

> *the core of his soul, the divine force in its depths, is capable of acting upon* [the soul], *changing it, binding the conflicting forces together, amalgamating the diverging elements—unifying it. This unification must be accomplished before a* [person] *undertakes some unusual work.* (148)

Asceticism, while it can help one to purify the soul, cannot protect it against inner contradiction.

So how, you may ask, does this unification begin? Buber believes that while the unification of the soul—of the whole person—is never final, any work done with genuine *kavana* (intention) only pulls the soul in the direction of a steadier unity. A person can, however, reach a unity that is great enough to allow him or her to effortlessly overcome contradictions. Wholeness begins with affirming your responsibility to yourself and to God for unifying your soul. Once you are able to affirm your whole self, you begin on the path to liberating the "divine spark" in your being that is enclosed by a shell or "crust" of separating individualism.

I vividly recall visiting professor K. J. Nishitani spending an entire graduate seminar at Temple University in the late sixties lecturing on and discussing just one Buddhist verse: "A person who is concentrated knows a thing as it really is." By "concentrated," Nishitani meant "gathered together at the center." He was fond of explaining that when one comes into a state of meditative concentration, or mindfulness, that person knows the "real reality" of a thing. For Buber, one's soul becomes unified—concentrated—only in the midst of becoming genuinely engaging and being engaged by another.

NATURE AND GRACE

Buber's commentary on this anecdote thus takes us to the heart of spiritual life by virtue of distinguishing between a person with a unified soul and one with a divided soul:

> *One* [person]—'*by nature' or 'by grace,' however one chooses to put it—has a unitary soul, a soul all of a piece, and accordingly performs unitary works, works all of a piece, because his soul, by being as it is, prompts and enables him*

to do so; another [person] *has a divided, complicated, contradictory soul, and this, naturally, affects his doings: their inhibitions and disturbances originate in the inhibitions and disturbances of his soul; its restlessness is expressed in their restlessness.* (148)

Buber's distinction between the unified and disunified soul corresponds with his major distinction between I-Thou and I-It. Buber distinguishes here between a unified soul and a disunified soul, as shown in the table below:

Table 3.1.

Unified Soul	Dis-unified Soul
Gathered Together	Divided
Concentrated	Conflicted
Amalgamated	Contradictory
All of a Piece	Vacillating

A person with a unified soul performs unified work. Conversely, a divided soul limits and restricts one's doings. Buber says that the divine force in its depths is capable of binding and amalgamating conflicting elements together. This is both challenging and reassuring. It means that a person with a divided soul is not helpless. If you feel at times conflicted, you can enter into conversation with the source of the unified soul and expressed through others that you meet. It is up to you, however, to intend the unification of your soul, to remain resolved that it will happen, and to trust that God, together with your intention, can bring it about.

Buber refers to the task of trying to unify your soul as "pulling yourself together":

What else can [one] *do than each time, in the middle of his doing, 'pull himself together,' as we say, that is, rally his vacillating soul and again and again, having rallied it, re-concentrate it upon the goal—and more over be ready, like the hasid in the story when pride touches him, to sacrifice the goal in order to save the soul?* (149)

"Pulling oneself together," however, requires a remarkable trust in God as the Eternal Partner who continually enables us, through nature by grace, to become more unified. Buber tells us that

the [person] *with the divided, complicated, contradictory soul is not helpless: the core of his soul, the divine force in its depths, is capable of acting upon it, changing it, binding the conflicting forces together, amalgamating the diverging elements—is capable of unifying it. This unification must be accomplished before* [one] *undertakes some unusual work.* (149)

The unified soul is both the result of God's activity within the core of the soul itself and our intentional turning toward dialogue with the world.

A RELAXED VIGILANCE

The attainment of the goal is therefore not an individual achievement. It is always, from Buber's perspective, relational. One becomes whole by becoming wholeheartedly present. Precisely because unifying the soul is a relational act, however, it can never be achieved completely and permanently:

> *One thing must of course not be lost sight of: unification of the soul is never final . . . But any work that I do with a united soul reacts upon my soul, acts in the direction of new and greater unification, leads me, though by all sorts of detours, to a steadier unity than was the preceding one. Thus* [one] *ultimately reaches a point where he can rely upon his soul, because its unity is now so great that it overcomes contradiction with effortless ease. Vigilance, of course, is necessary even then, but it is a relaxed vigilance.* (150)

Buber views the means (entering into dialogue) and the goal (a unified soul) as mutually reciprocal and mutually reinforcing. Anything that we do with a unified soul, as a fully present whole person, renews our soul's unification and strengthens us on our own path.

It is as a result of the divine-human partnership, then, that the "*steadier unity*" of one's soul is achieved. Our responsibility is to enter each thing we do as unified as we possibly can be. If we do this from our side of the divine-human relationship, the main work is accomplished. The spirit acts upon our soul and leads it to greater unification. For this to happen, however, what Buber calls a "relaxed vigilance" is necessary.

It is crucial to understand what Buber means by the seemingly contradictory phrase "relaxed vigilance." The term itself arises from Buber's understanding of what it means to be a whole person in body, mind, and spirit. In his classic *I and Thou*, he suggests that the action of the whole person means the suspension of all partial actions and of all conflicting sensations. And then he adds, reflecting his deep appreciation for the Taoist tradition, that the activity of the person with a unified soul looks like "doing nothing" in that nothing separate or partial stirs the person to activity. By "doing nothing," or "not-doing," Buber meant to suggest an activity entered into by the fully present person. It is this type of calm and self-contained action that Buber calls relaxed vigilance.

We need to be careful here. Like soul-unification itself, relaxed vigilance is not a state that we finally achieve. Nor is it a condition that we come to possess. Maurice Friedman, for example, in a 1996 unpublished interview on the educational process said:

> In *The Way of Man* Buber speaks of "resolution" as part of becoming whole. "We never really become whole," he says, "but we can reach the place of relaxed vigilance." I've observed that every time I reach that stage it falls through.

Why? For one reason, when we step back to observe our self, we remove our self from surrendering into relationship. For another reason, "relaxed vigilance" is not a place, or state of consciousness, or achievement, but the not-doing doing in which action appears like doing nothing special because it does not interfere or intervene but flows with what is done. To the person who is fully present in relationship, the notion of "relaxed vigilance" as a separate idea disappears along with self-reflective awareness of the one who observes it.

WHAT DO I NEED TO KNOW?

Buber's interpretation of this Hasidic tale opens us to a relational strategy at the heart of Hasidism—we need divine assistance and, simultaneously, God needs us to do everything possible to pull ourselves together. If Buber were giving this talk today, he might well repeat a central theme from his classic *I and Thou*: God does not ask for our dependence, but for a partnership that exists on both sides of the divine-human relationship. It is our *partnership* with God that makes possible every meaningful relation to the world. God is always, according to Buber, ready to enter into a partnership with anyone who turns with his or her whole being towards the divine voice. We might imagine God, if we must imagine God as anything, as the perfect listener: someone who not only hears every word, but also hears our thoughts, even those we are not yet aware of; one who completely understands what we mean by everything that we say and don't say; and one who always responds honestly, compassionately, and justly.

> You know always in your heart that you need God more than everything; but do you not know too that God needs you—in the fullness of His eternity needs you? How would man be, how would you be, if God did not need him, did not need you? You need God, in order to be—and God needs you, for the very meaning of your life. In instruction and in poems men are at pains to say more, and they say too much—what turgid and presumptuous talk that is about the "God who

becomes"; but we know unshakably in our hearts that there is a becoming of a God that is. The world is not divine sport, it is divine destiny. There is a divine meaning in the life of the world, of man, of human persons, of you and of me.[6]

Impossible to understand, yet necessary to imagine, God needs my cooperative participation for our partnership to flourish.

We hear again echoes of Buber's basic life-insight here—that our relationship to God, when genuine, and our relationship to each other, when genuine, is powerfully bonded and spiritually redemptive. These relationships are not just connected, not just associated, but flow from, and are motivated by, the same spirit, and it is the dynamic reciprocity of the divine-human partnership that unifies us. I intend it; I will it; I practice it. God creates the opportunity; God bestows the inspiration to do it; God graces the relationship. It is the transformative spirit of a common fruitfulness and elemental togetherness that joins us in communion both to one another and to God. A unified soul is born and nurtured by the power of this uniquely reciprocal relationship between God and yourself.

A DIFFICULTY

When Buber subjects the tale to deeper scrutiny, a contradiction arises, however. Buber says that the divided soul is capable of being unified—being acted upon by the divine force in the soul's depths—but he also says that this unification should be accomplished prior to undertaking some unusual spiritual work. Only with a unified soul—a soul all of a piece—will one be able to successfully achieve one's work, but one's very work is the act of unifying the soul. Is Buber speaking here, one may wonder, only about "spiritual" work or about any undertaking that is of value?

For a moment, suppose that Buber is right—that the unification of the soul "can never be achieved in the middle of the work." Our souls must be unified from the beginning if our actions are to bear ripe fruit. Implied in this statement is another spiritual principal—We cannot achieve unification merely through a method or practice that we apply, use, or imitate. Many practitioners of Buddhist meditative traditions wrestle with a similar problem: Can one attain awakening by practicing sitting or does the practitioner need to be awakened first before knowing how to practice? In Japanese Soto Zen Buddhism, for example, meditation is the practice of just sitting without seeking enlightenment, and there should be no thought of awakening at all in one's practice. To sit in meditation is itself the realization of Zen practice. In western monastic traditions, the practice of asceticism (e.g., deprivation of food, or drink, or sleep) is employed.

Buber offers us a pathway through this conundrum between practicing a spiritual method to become unified and the need to be unified before undertaking any spiritual practice. While asceticism, Buber writes, can purify and concentrate the soul, its achievements cannot be preserved intact until the goal is attained. Why? Because asceticism cannot protect the soul from its own contradiction. To think of the unified soul as a concept or ideal or as the content of my/our own experience is to miss its deep recesses of meaning. The unified soul—the whole person—is not fully present unless it engages the other, whether the other is person, place, or thing.

WHOLENESS

According to Buber, the "real I" becomes present as I bring the ever-changing, never-having-before-been, and always-new spirit that I uniquely embody into engagement with others. Buber consistently refers to the question of personal presence by insisting on the wholeness of the human person. "Wholeness," for him, refers to a seamless integration of body, mind, heart and spirit. According to Buber, human wholeness includes our place in the cosmos, our connection with destiny, our relation to the world, our understanding of the other, our attitude towards the mystery of life's encounters, and our awareness of our own death. But how is this "wholeness" manifested? Is it really possible to become a "whole person"?

It is not at all possible if one thinks that Buber means by our becoming whole that we can take some action or set of actions that makes us become whole. Nor is personal wholeness a once-and-for-all state of being. Rather than a precondition for happiness that we can attain or the abstract content of our beliefs, wholeness is a direction of movement that comes and goes in particular concrete moments. By "wholeness," Buber meant both "choosing" to enter relationship and "being chosen" by one who also chooses to enter relationship. In other words, wholeness involves both surrender and action, grace and will, and mutuality.

Because "wholeness" is actualized in genuine moments of engaging and being engaged, the phrase "whole person" means responding to others with all our bodily energies united, withholding nothing and leaving nothing out, and doing so "with all the available forces of my soul without conflict." In a healthy interplay between persons, "wholeness" embodies the presence of freedom. But the attainment of the goal is not an individual achievement. It is always, from Buber's perspective, a relational one. I become whole by truly entering into engagement with the world, with others, with God. When Buber writes that the "unification of the soul is never final," he means that we should not hold to a linear or sequential view of means and goal, but that we should view the means and the goal as mutually reciprocal and mutually reinforcing. Anything that we do with a unified soul, as a whole and fully present person, renews the soul's unification. Therefore, Buber says that when we become a unit of body and spirit, then our work is all of a piece.

To the extent that we separate and keep apart means and goal, practice and unification, attainment remains elusive. To the extent that we bring means and goal into a mutually up-building, interpenetrating relationship, attainment is not different from our daily activities. Practice, when the one who practices is fully present, is not different from attainment.

BUBER LIFE ANECDOTE

The autobiographical fragment that best exemplifies Buber's wisdom in this talk comes from early in his life. In this anecdote, Buber ponders a piece of mica:

> On a gloomy morning I walked upon the highway, saw a piece of mica lying, lifted it up and looked at it for a long time; the day was no longer gloomy, so much light was caught in the stone. And suddenly as I raised my eyes from it, I realized that while I looked I had not been conscious of "object" and "subject"; in my looking the mica and "I" had been one; in my looking I had tasted unity. I looked at it again, the unity did not return. But there it burned in me as though to create. I closed my eyes, I gathered my strength, I bound myself with my object, I raised the mica into the kingdom of the existing. And there . . . I first felt: I, there I first was I. The one who looked had not yet been I; only this man here, this unified man, bore the name like a crown. Now I perceived that first unity as the marble statue may perceive the block out of which it was chiseled; it was the undifferentiated, I was the unification. Still I did not understand myself; but then there flashed through me the memory: thus had my body fifteen human years before done the simple deed and, the fingers entwined, united life and death to "I."[7]

In this extraordinary experience, while looking at a piece of mica, the young Buber suddenly "tasted unity" by realizing that he was momentarily not conscious of subject or object. Years later, in hindsight Buber could say that "I was the unification."

A few years later, in *I and Thou*, Buber would recall this event:

> So much can never break through the crust of the condition of things! O fragment of mica, looking on which I once learned, for the first time, that I is not something "in me"—with you I was nevertheless only bound up in myself; at that time the event took place only in me, not between me and you. But when one

that is alive rises out of things, and becomes a being in relation to me, joined to me by its nearness and its speech, for how inevitably short a time it is nothing to me but Thou! It is not the relation that necessarily grows feeble, but the actuality of its immediacy.[8]

While looking at the "fragment of mica," Buber makes the powerful discovery that the *"I"* is not something *"in me."* Rather, the "real *I*," my true self, emerges in "genuine dialogue," in presentness, freedom, direction, and mutuality. This dialogical realization sets Buber apart from philosophers for whom the "I" is known primarily *within* the self. Of course, the idea that we become ourselves most genuinely in relation does imply that we owe our ability to become human to *relationship* itself, that we should depend on our existence on a single human relationship. Our foremost task is to fulfill our unique, unpredictable, never-recurring potentialities by hallowing the everyday with others, not to depend on others for our sense of wholeness.

CLOSING TALE

In Buber's words,

Unification of the soul would be thoroughly misunderstood if 'soul' were taken to mean anything but the whole [person], body and spirit together. The soul is not really united, unless all bodily energies, all the limbs of the body, are united. (150)

Buber reinforces this point by closing with a Hasidic tale in which Rabbi Nahum enters the house of study when he was not expected only to find his disciples playing checkers. If you are like me, you may find this tale easy to identify with. When they saw the rabbi, they were embarrassed to be "caught" playing a board game instead of studying the Torah, and they stopped what they were doing. Here is the full tale:

On one of the days of the Hanukkah feast, Rabbi Nahum, the son of the rabbi of Rishyn [district of Kiev], entered the House of Study at a time when he was not expected, and found his disciples playing checkers, as was the custom on those days. When they saw the zaddik they were embarrassed and stopped playing. But he gave them a kindly nod and asked: 'Do you know the rules of the game of checkers?' And when they did not reply for shyness he himself gave the answer: 'I shall tell you the rules of the game of checkers. The first is that one must not make two moves at once. The second is that one may only move forward and not backward. And the third is that when one has reached the last row, one may move wherever one likes.' (150–51)

When you attain the spiritual goal, as St. Augustine once said, "you love God and do as you please." Therefore, even playing a game of checkers can become a part of finding one's way on the spiritual path if it is played with a unified soul. This is why, according to Buber, the Baal-Shem interpreted the scriptural passage "Whatsoever thy hands find to do, do it with [all] thy might" the way he did, as a challenge to unify one's soul. That is to say, when we become whole, when there is no part of our remaining outside of our actions, then we become a unit of body and spirit. Whatever we do thereafter is done all of a piece.

PRACTICE EXERCISES

I. Chapter-Specific Questions

(Designed to bring greater clarity to Buber's central insights.)

1. Why did the rabbi of Lublin designate the Hasid's struggle with fasting as "patchwork?" Do you agree with him or not? Do you believe that fasting can be a way to reach God? What does Buber say about the Hasid's choice to fast? Does he condone fasting as a way to reach God? Why or why not?
2. What elements of your soul are in conflict? What do you vacillate over? How do you imagine reversing this situation?
3. How do you experience Rabbi Nahum's three rules of checkers—one move at a time; only move forward; from the last row move anywhere in your life?
4. Do you agree with Buber that it is necessary to unify your soul before attempting any significant task? If not, why?

II. Comparative Questions

(Designed to deepen your dialogue with Buber's spiritual techniques.)

1. Now and then a question addresses you with a different urgency without needing an immediate answer. Looking back at these specific questions, select one that would be helpful to live with without yet having a clear answer. Are you willing to live within a question, so to speak, and allow its echoes, its implications, its edges to affect the way you relate to the world? What happens to that question when you bring it, unanswered, into your discourse? When is the time right to return to the question and allow an answer to form itself for you?

2. What is the key element of this third talk, the central insight upon which the entire presentation is based? How does it challenge you? Imagine yourself in a conversation with Buber about one of these questions which most challenges you or which most surprises you. What do you think Buber would say? In response, what would you say to Buber?

3. Following Buber's interpretation of the Hasidic tradition in this presentation, what practice could you initiate, or intensify, in your life that would embody this understanding? What is the first thing you would do? Then what?

4. What does the dynamic relation between rebbe and disciple indicate about the disciple's behavior? With whom do you most identify in this story? How would you have acted either similarly or differently than the disciple?

III. Feedback Questions

(Designed to help you achieve life-integrations in meaningful dialogue with others.)

1. Select a question from the Chapter-Specific and Comparative Questions above. After engaging that question in dialogue with another person, what new insights and understandings emerged from the conversation?

2. Of the various responses you have made in your journal, which one is of the greatest value to you where you are standing in life right now? How might you integrate your response into your daily life?

3. Have a dialogue in writing with Buber in which you ask a heartfelt question and then listen to hear Buber's response as if it was aimed uniquely at you. Before writing down "Buber's" answer, listen quietly to allow what he might say to form itself in your mind. Later, you may wish to share your dialogue script with someone.

4. Try to notice how your most pressing life-question and the way you have been answering it changes your dialogical relationships with others. What did you come to realize as a result of these dialogues? Record what you notice as you reflect on your meetings with others at the end of a day.

Part II

Practicing Presentness

Chapter 4

Beginning with Yourself

"Everything depends on myself, and the crucial decision: I will straighten myself out." (158)

SUMMARY OF BUBER'S FOURTH TALK

In the fourth talk, "Beginning with Oneself," Buber shifts from discussing preliminary movements necessary to experience along the spiritual path to actions of a fulfilled existence. Indeed, the fourth presentation has more of a therapeutic emphasis than the others. Buber believes that to advance spiritually one must "begin with oneself," not in the sense of adopting an elevated self-importance but in the sense of taking complete responsibility for one's actions and words in the world. While not to be taken as the goal in itself, searching for the center of the self should become one's starting-point. Buber then illuminates the Hasidic teaching about the origin of conflict. Hasidic teachings envision the fundamental structure of each person as a whole. Overcoming external conflict requires engaging with internal conflict. For the Baal-Shem-Tov, "The origin of all conflicts between me and my fellow men is that I do not say what I mean and that I do not do what I say." Accordingly, the fundamental source of external conflict is an internal inconsistency between thoughts and words, between attitudes and feelings, and between beliefs and doubts. One needs to come to the crucial realization that "everything depends on myself." Essentially, to advance spiritually, you must begin with yourself, not with the trivial ego but with the deeper self, by taking full responsibility for your part in conflict-situations, by harmonizing your thought, speech, and action, and by saying what you mean and doing what you say.

55

OPENING HASIDIC TALE

Buber begins his fourth talk by relating a tale about one Rabbi giving advice
to another.

*Once when Rabbi Yitzhak of Vorki was playing host to certain prominent men
of Israel, they discussed the value to a household of an honest and efficient
servant. They said that a good servant made for good management and cited
Joseph at whose hands everything prospered. Rabbi Yitzhak objected. 'I once
thought that too,' he said. 'But then my teacher showed me that everything
depends on the master of the house. You see, in my youth my wife gave me a
great deal of trouble, and though I myself put up with her as best I could, I was
sorry for the servants. So I went to my teacher, Rabbi David of Lelov, and asked
him whether I should oppose my wife. All he said was: "Why do you speak to
me? Speak to yourself!" I thought over these words for quite a while before I
understood them. But I did understand them when I recalled a certain saying
of the Baal-Shem: "There is thought, speech and action. Thought corresponds
to one's wife, speech to one's children, and action to one's servants. Whoever
straightens himself out in regard to all three will find that everything prospers
at his hands." Then I understood what my teacher had meant: everything de-
pended on myself.'(154–55)*

KEY TEACHINGS AND PRACTICES

Why wasn't the fourth tale, we might reasonably ask, placed first since it
focuses on "Beginning With Oneself"? The answer, I believe, may be found
in the basic two-part structure of Buber's six talks. His series of talks began
with a discussion of preliminary practices that prepare us for our spiritual
journey (in chapters 1–3). Buber then moves (in chapters 4–6) to a discussion
of what it means to participate fully, presently, and dialogically in redemption. The first three talks speak of the need for the spiritual traveler to slow
down long enough to concentrate his or her willpower on moving ahead
toward the life of dialogue. As we retreat ahead of our habitual fears and
resistance, we begin to see before us the possibility of genuine dialogue in all
of our encounters. In other words, the organization of Buber's talks suggests,
the preliminary practices of *heart-searching, your particular way,* and *resolution* set the stage for the practices of *beginning, turning,* and *standing-here.*

It is necessary for the soil to be prepared so that the seeds that are planted
will take root, so the first three talks describe the conditions, intentions, and
actions necessarily as we begin our spiritual journey. They ask the question: Are you ready to prepare yourself to let God in? In the first talk, Buber

reminded us that God—the biblical God who is also the ever-unique, ever-personal, ever-listening, ever-dialogical, and ever-loving and who manifests to us in each moment—addresses you personally as Thou with this question: "Where are you?" Before we begin to make a dwelling-place for God, God asks us, through the encounters of our daily lives, how far along have we proceeded in our life and where we stand right now.

In the second talk, Buber reminded us of our particular task, which is for each of us to find our ever-unique, never-having-been, never-to-be-repeated way of serving God. Since we are all called into conversation with God in unique ways, following what speaks to your heart in manner that honors both tradition and the specificity of your own calling is a second preliminary step toward letting God in and hallowing the everyday.

In his third talk, Buber underscored this division between his first three and the last three talks. When commenting on the Hasid's attempted fast, Buber indicated that the Seer of Lublin believed that fasting could help lift the Hasid's soul to a higher rung in the initial stage of a person's development. What becomes apparent here is that it is important to overcome, before beginning, those things that can hinder us from accomplishing our purpose. To accomplish any great task with your whole self it is necessary to unify your soul—the divine force of your innermost being. Before beginning, therefore, you are to re-concentrate your efforts upon the goal with a unified body, mind, and spirit.

YOU ARE NEVER ALONE

But how can the soul that is conflicted and divided become unified? For Buber, we must rely neither on God's healing grace nor on human action alone but on their reciprocal and reciprocating partnership. On the one hand, at the deepest core of the soul the divine force binds the conflicting forces together, amalgamating the divergent elements of ourselves. This unification cannot be brought about solely by human effort.

Still, it may be beneficial, for some, to begin the journey toward genuine dialogue with practices of detachment, abstinence, and self-isolation to achieve a certain amount of liberation from enslavements to the world. Asceticism, however, although it can purify and concentrate the soul at times, cannot preserve its achievements and cannot make the soul overcome its own contradictions. The soul's unification is never final, and inner difficulties inevitably arise. Yet whatever work I accomplish with a unified soul reinforces my soul's unity and leads in the direction of a "new and greater unification . . . to a *steadier* unity than was the preceding one."

Before we begin, it is necessary to search our hearts (Do you believe that God is asking you to enter into dialogue?), to recognize and to choose our own particular way of entering into dialogue (Do you believe it is even possible with all of your strength and without imitating what others have done?), and to pull yourself together (What are the sources of your disunity?). Only then are we ready to undertake the unusual work of hallowing our relationship to God, to the world, to others, and to ourselves with our whole being.

WHAT IS THE ORIGIN OF CONFLICT?

The story of Rabbi Yitzhak of Vorki that opens the first talk touches upon one of life's deepest problems: the origin of conflict between persons. Conflict may result from either conscious motives (such as the desire to "win" an argument) or from the unconscious complexes to which these motives relate. From a Hasidic perspective, conflict arises from our inner being and can only be resolved through the transformation of one's basic stance in the world. In order to resolve conflict, according to Hasidic teaching, we must seek real transformation, first of ourselves and then of our relationships. Rather than exploring the psychic elements of the conflict, as one might in therapy, the resolution of conflict is achieved by the comprehensive effort of the person as a whole.

The *practical* Hasidic teaching contends that rather than focusing on the object of the conflict, which, after all, tends to prolong the conflict in the first place, each person is called upon to straighten him- or herself out. Conflicts with others are the effects of conflict within our own soul.

> At first, [a person] *should realize that conflict-situations between* [oneself] *and others are nothing but the effects of conflict-situations in* [one's] *own soul. Then* [one] *should try to overcome this inner conflict, so that afterwards* [one] *may go out to* [other people] *and enter into new, transformed relationships with them.* (156–57)

We need to overcome our internal conflicts before we see a decisive reversal. Or, as Rabbi Bunam taught, we must learn to "Seek peace in your own place." The Baal-Shem taught that to overcome conflict one needs to straighten oneself out in three areas: (1) thought, (2) speech, and (3) action. The conflict between these three principles leads Buber to encapsulate Hasidic teaching on this subject with a memorable remark:

> *The origin of all conflict between me and* [others] *is that I do not say what I mean, and I do not do what I say. For this confuses and poisons, again and*

again and in increasing measure, the situation between myself and the other [person]. (158)

Intention by itself is not enough. It also must include follow-through. Yet in order to say what I mean and do what I say I must also straighten myself out. One can straighten one's self out in the areas of thought, speech, and action, beginning to do what one says and say what one means. The crucial realization here, though, is that everything depends on me, that, as two-sided as my conflicts may seem, only *I* can resolve them. This can be accomplished by finding "the deeper self of the person living in a relationship to the world." Thus, Rabbi David of Lelov says "Why do you speak to me? Speak to yourself!"

FROM CONFLICT TO CONTACT

In Buber's words, Hasidic teaching attributes external conflict to internal disunity. At the same time, you must begin with yourself but not aim at yourself. You must straighten yourself out before you can find any answers and before you can engage in genuine relationship with others. You must unify yourself and take yourself as a whole, all together. It won't help much to begin picking apart the origins of your conflicts piece by piece. One thing is not more important than another. Each thing is a "starting point" from which we can begin to address the whole.

When I was working on sections of this chapter, for instance, I met a therapist at my health club, a couples' counselor. Together with his wife, Charlie has lectured, taught, and led workshops on committed relationships around the world. We had talked once before about my enthusiasm for Buber's philosophy of dialogue and more specifically its implications for dialogical psychotherapy. In fact, he was about to travel East to lead a weekend workshop called "From Conflict to Contact." When I heard that title, I said: "For Buber, the real source of conflict between persons is always and only one's self."

"Yes," he said, smiling "that's right. Each person must take responsibility for the problems that block real relationship."

"Yes," I said. "For Buber we are just wasting our energy when we blame others for breakdowns."

"True, we only spread around more chaos," he affirmed, "which makes it harder and harder to clean it up."

Listening attentively, he made me feel that what I was saying was valuable. His listening led me to ask, "I'm curious about what method you encourage workshop participants to practice. If you were to choose just one method for shifting relationships from conflict to contact, what would it be?"

After a brief pause, he said, "A tried and true one—taking a 'time out.' I suggest that each person stop fighting for a moment and quietly think about what they are doing."

This simple method reverberated with me for much of that afternoon while I was working on this chapter. I wondered how Buber would address conflicts between couples in a practical manner? I wondered what he would say.

The next time I saw Charlie at the health club, I had a surprise for him—a one-page outline of what Buber might say to workshop participants. It seemed reasonable to me that he would affirm two preliminary points—one about the source of conflict and one about the source of contact:

1. "The origin of all conflict between persons is that I do not say what I mean, and that I do not do what I say."
2. Genuine dialogue is healing "between partners who have turned to one another in truth, who express themselves without reserve and are free of [agendas]."

Taking full responsibility for your/myself means facing up to the consequences of our actions, especially when they lead to disharmony. Yet taking responsibility how? By turning towards and surrendering into mutual, open, honest, dialogue. Genuine dialogue, Buber would say, is the beginning of the healing process. It's up to each person to effect that healing through reciprocally addressing and responding, speaking and listening, challenging and being challenged.

The focus of the sheet that I handed him contained a four-fold Buberian way of responding to conflicts:

1. Problem
   • Elevating "I" over "We"
   • Needing to look good and be right
   • Blaming and judging the other for the conflict
2. Solution
   • Realizing the origin of conflict is within me
   • Experiencing trust, caring, and support of the other
   • Mutual confirmation of the other
3. Method
   • Mutually agreed-upon retreating temporarily to reflect on my responsibility
   • Returning to dialogue with the partner to discuss my responsibility
   • Responding with support for my partner's expression of responsibility

4. Results
    *   Mutually supportive contact
    *   Deepened love, trust, and commitment
    *   Grounding practice for future conflicts

When he read it, a bright smile lit his face. "That's wonderful," he said. "People should see it. People should practice it!"[1]

THE TWO I'S

Why, in Hasidic teaching, must a person recognize that interpersonal conflict is nothing but the effects of conflict within one's own soul? Because seeing oneself as "an individual contrasted with other individuals" keeps us separate from each other and prevents us from being "genuine persons." Each "genuine person's" transformation "helps towards the transformation of the world." If you "begin with yourself" you are able to arrive at transformation. In fact, all we are really able to do is begin with ourselves, to start from where we are, in own places, from what is possible and real for us.

If everything depends on my making the crucial decision to straighten myself out so that I can enter into genuine relationships, how is this to be accomplished? According to Buber, I must be able to find my way from "the trivial ego of the egoistic individual" to "the deeper self of the person living in a relationship to the world." What Buber means here by "trivial ego" is clearly illustrated by a note I recently received from a friend.

> I wish at times like now that I could overcome my competitive resentment toward others who I assume are succeeding more than I, thus placing me in the pit of adolescent victimization. It is immature as hell, and yet, I find myself getting sucked into it. Perhaps, there is a lack of social reinforcement, which is only partially true. I need to get a better hold on myself at this stage of my life, to present myself both to myself and others in a more forthright, subtle, loving, and intuitive manner. I also recognize that I am capable of doing so, but slide too easily given any downward turn.[2]

In our time, the "I" of the little self has become "gigantically swollen" and is thus unable to recognize its own real nature. How Buber characterizes the identity, manifestation, and redemptive significance of what he calls the "real I"—genuine wholeness and the interhuman way—is the subject of these remarks.

If we are to begin with ourselves, we might ask, "Of what does the self consist?" The formation of the "I," according to Buber, involves two basic relationships to the world, or two fundamentally different modes of self-expression that appear in the same person. Buber describes the little "I" as a self-willed individual who relates to the world as an *It*. In *I and Thou* Buber writes, "The *I* of the primary word *I-It* makes its appearance as individuality and becomes conscious of itself as subject (of experiencing and using)."[3] On the other hand, Buber describes the "real I" as an open, other-directed, relational person. If an "individual," by definition, remains separate from other individuals, a "person" is one who enters into relationship with others. The former breaks away; the latter seeks interrelatedness. The relational person lives not through "experiencing" and "using," but through engaging and being engaged.

Table 4.1.

Individual	Person
Ego-oriented; Separated from Others	Relationship-oriented; with Others
Breaks away from Relational Events	Seeks Interrelation
Experiences and Uses	Realizes Contact with Others
Characterized by Self-consciousness	Characterized by Turning-towards
Being-So-and-None-Other	Becoming Dialogical

Whereas the isolated "individual" is concerned with his or her "me-ness"— his or her accomplishments, experiences, affiliations, and genius, the "real *I*" is nothing more, and nothing less, than a "dialogical person" who spontaneously, freely, and directly enters into real relationships.

It is impossible, however, to make peace and enter into dialogue with others unless you make peace with yourself. This is not a task that can be forced and then finished forever. This is an ongoing task that, as it renews itself, renews your ability to connect with and engage in real relationship with others.

DECISIVE REVERSAL

While Buber agrees that external problems often derive from internal causes, he also notes that Hasidic teaching does not explore particular psychical complications, dynamics, or ailments, but instead envisions the person as a whole. Hasidism is less concerned with internal compulsions and unconscious drives than with the whole person. Real transformation, Buber says, and real restoration—at first of the single person, then of the relationship—is achieved by comprehending this whole.

"Wholeness," as discussed in the third lecture, refers to a seamless integration of body, mind, and spirit. According to Buber, human wholeness includes:

- our place in the cosmos,
- our connection with destiny,
- our relation to the world,
- our understanding of the other,
- our attitude towards the mystery of life's encounters, and
- our awareness of our own death.

Because "wholeness" is actualized in genuine moments of meeting, the phrase "whole person" indicates a direction of movement rather than the content of a belief. It suggests for Buber not only one's spiritual unification but one's unique presence as well. Personal wholeness always embodies a unique direction of movement along with a unique response to each concrete situation. Buber summarizes what he means by wholeness in dialogue as follows:

> *With the whole being can be described most simply thus: I enter into the act or event which is in question with all the available forces of my soul without conflict, without even latent much less perceptible conflict.*[4]

STRAIGHTEN YOURSELF OUT

Buber's emphasis on Hasidism's challenge to "straighten yourself out" is like a neon arrow pointing directly to the place we must go to resolve conflict, to the place where conflict begins. Starting with yourself does not mean taking aim at yourself, though; rather, it means being willing to take responsibility for the consequences of your actions in the world. Trying to avoid dealing with conflict, or focusing only on the elements we believe to have caused a conflict, are both doomed strategies. Such approaches are limited by a perspective in which one sees oneself as an individual contrasted with other individuals and not as a whole person in relation to others. Therefore, "The essential thing is to begin with oneself, and at this moment a [person] has nothing in the world to care about [other] than this beginning." (28; 156)

In the words of Rabbi Bunam,

> *'Our sages say: "Seek peace in your own place." You cannot find peace anywhere save in your own self. In the psalm we read: "There is no peace in my bones because of my sin." When a [person] has made peace within himself he will be able to make peace in the whole world.'* (157)

In order to find peace within ourselves, three principles of our being—our thoughts, our words, and our actions—need to be united. It is important that these are united, in Buber's words, because not saying what I mean and doing what I say

> *confuses and poisons, again and again and in increasing measure, the situation between myself and the other* [person], *and I, in my internal disintegration, am no longer able to master it but, contrary to all my illusions, have become its slave.* (157)

By not saying what we mean, by not doing what we say, we open ourselves to further conflict:

> *By our contradiction, our lie, we foster conflict-situations and give them power over us until they enslave us. From here, there is no way out but by the crucial realization: Everything depends on myself, and the crucial decision: I will straighten myself out.* (158)

But to do this, as we have seen, to reverse conflict between myself and the world, it is necessary to find my whole self as person, to find the way out from the "trivial ego" to the "deeper self" of the person living in a relationship to the world.

PAULA

By "beginning with yourself," Buber means more than just believing in yourself or learning to trust and accept yourself. Rather, he means answering for ourselves. Buber's compelling essay on Soren Kierkegaard bears the provocative motto "Responsibility is the navel-string of creation.—P. B."[5] "P. B." was Buber's wife of more than 50 years, Paula, his consummate dialogical partner. A highly intellectual woman, Paula wrote novels in German under the pseudonym Georg Munk. Through his loving relationship with Paula, Buber learned true responsibility.

What Buber writes about a genuine person could not have been formulated, as Buber noted himself, without the creative support and unconditional love of Paula. Buber's relationship to Paula was of crucial importance for his life's work. In the summer of 1899, while attending the University of Zurich, Buber met Paula Winkler, and they married shortly in spite of objections that she was a Gentile—"a pagan," as she joked. Although raised a Munich Catholic, she converted to Judaism, and in so doing lost her own family. Remarkably, as Hugo Bergmann observed, when Paula said "we Jews," "we felt ourselves confirmed." In Paula, Martin found true equality of relationship. With Paula, Buber came to recognize that marriage is built upon mutually saying what you mean and doing what you say. In his poem "Do You Still Know It?" written in 1949 to commemorate their 50 years of life together, Buber credited Paula with helping him find direction for his talents and interests. In it, he wrote two lines that link genuine dialogue with transcendence:

> *How a mutual animated describing*
> *Arose out of it and lived between you and me!*[6]

The phrase "mutual animated describing" points directly to what Buber meant by sacramental dialogue that emerges from "the between."

Paula and Martin's life together was one of mutual responsibility. Undoubtedly, he had her in mind when he talked about a person's taking responsibility for life, for one's own actions. For this reason, Buber said that "genuine responsibility" exists precisely in moments of "real responding." But responding to what?

> *To what happens to one, to what is to be seen and heard and felt. Each concrete hour allotted to the person, with its content drawn from the word and from destiny, is speech for the* [person] *who is attentive.*[7]

The truly attentive person participates in the creative process as it occurs, that is, we are addressed—spoken to—by sounds, voices, images, words, events in and through our everyday environment.

> *A newly-created reality has been laid in our arms; we answer for it. A dog has looked at you, you answer for its glance, a child has clutched your hand, you answer for its touch, a host of* [persons] *move about you, you answer for their need.*[8]

Being fully responsible in each new situation for Buber meant responding uniquely and spontaneously from the depths of your personality. Buber did not accept an ethic of responsibility based on once-for-all dogmatic positions of political, educational, or religious traditions. Each situation presents you with an unforeseeable moment that calls for a unique decision. The spiritual technology of "beginning," therefore, involves starting with your whole self (the unified soul of the last talk) and taking full responsibility for the polarized patchwork of conflicts in your life. Acting responsibly depends on yourself, depends on realizing and expressing your deeper self. By so doing, you not only transform yourself, you transform as well that part of the world in which you are situated.

BEGINNING

Not surprisingly, an episode in Buber's own life perfectly exemplifies this practice of beginning with ourselves. Recall Buber's being overwhelmed while reading the Baal-Shem-Tov as a younger man. Do you remember how he responded?

> *It was then that, overpowered in an instant, I experienced the Hasidic soul. The primally Jewish opened to me, flowering to newly conscious expression in the darkness of exile:* [our] *being created in the image of God I grasped as deed, as becoming, as task.*[9]

Acting in consort with God, as for the Baal-Shem-Tov, it now became Buber's task, goal, intention, life-direction, unifying purpose, Buber's deed, action in the world, creative, vocational accomplishment, and Buber's becoming always new in relationship with others.

But there's more. By beginning with yourself Buber also means beginning with your relationship to God and to others. On October 31, 1951, Buber flew from Israel to New York with his wife Paula to begin a large lecture tour on both coasts of the United States. In his early seventies, between 1951 and 1952, Buber gave 73 lectures, 3 of which he gave on Judaism at the Jewish Theological Seminary in New York, partly out of desire to meet the next generation of the faithful. Holding that Hasidic teaching was the consummation of Judaism, in a lecture titled "The Silent Question," Buber made an impassioned statement:

> *For the sake of this your beginning, God created the world. He has drawn it out of himself so that you may bring it closer to Him. Meet the world with the fullness of your being and you shall meet Him. That He Himself accepts from your hands what you have to give the world, is His Mercy. If you wish to believe, love!*[10]

In other words, your life will remain incomplete if you yourself do not begin on your path with a spirit of active love.

For Buber, God created the world so that you and I could begin with ourselves by entering into loving engagement with the world. Love, here, is not an inner feeling but a two-sided relationship in which you experience those you meet in the world from their own side of the relationship. Beginning with yourself, therefore, does not mean ending with yourself. As we will hear Buber say in his next talk, beginning with yourself is fulfilled only when you turn away from yourself toward another, the world, and/or God. Beginning with myself, in other words, is completed—brought to its highest fruition—in the practice of turning fully and dialogically toward whomever and whatever I encounter.

IMAGE AND LIKENESS

Buber's understanding that God created the world for the sake of our beginning provided him with a specific, life-long spiritual practice. This practice emerged from his understanding of two verses from the account of the creation in the book of Genesis:

> Then God said, "Let us make [human beings] in our image, after our likeness, to have dominion over the fish in the sea, the birds of the air, the cattle, all wild animals on land, and everything that creeps on the earth." (Genesis 1:26)

In this first verse, God is going to create humans in God's own likeness. But God ultimately, in the very next verse, creates humans only in the *image* of God: "in the image of God He created them. Male and female He created them" (Genesis 1:27). Had God abandoned the first divine covenant? This discrepancy challenged Buber to the core.

When Buber considered what the ancient Rabbis said about the discrepancy between these two verses, it became more and more apparent to him that he was being addressed by this question personally. Buber found one provocative answer to the conundrum in a rabbinic interpretation: Likeness lies in the hands of humans. What Adam had failed to do, to work on himself so that he would be worthy of God's likeness, Buber now felt called to rectify. Buber felt called to carry forth Adam's task, but had yet to discover what that task was. In Buber's mind, Adam mistook God's original intention in creation. Adam didn't realize that he had to work toward perfecting the image of God placed inside him.

Buber came to realize that this is the task of everyone who recognizes God's address to them. The task is to become a partner *with* God in creation, a co-author of God's plan. God's creation is always unfinished without our participation in it. The spiritual practice arising from this realization—simple, yet profound—occurs in each moment of honest, open, mutual, present relationship. In this practice, for Buber, we become co-creators in God's ongoing creation of all existence and help to fulfill God's original intention of creating us in the likeness of the divine source.

BUBER LIFE ANECDOTE

The following sketch illustrates what occurred for Buber when he began with himself, with his own interests, curiosities, and what affected him the most. Buber spent his first year of university in Vienna listening to lectures by significant scholars. Yet, as he reports, they did not have a decisive effect on him. There were, however, some small seminars into which he flung himself that did exert a strong influence upon him. As he reports, the interactions between teacher and students in these seminars affected him "more intimately than anything that I read in a book" because they were infused with the spirit of direct speech and of the "between." In other words beginning with yourself for Buber is beginning with what we all have in common—meaningful speech, *dia-logos*.

What affected me most strongly, however, was the Burgtheater into which at times, day after day, I rushed up three flights after several hours of "posting myself" in order to capture a place in the highest gallery. When far below in front of me the curtain went up and I might then look at the events of the dramatic agon as, even if in play, taking here and now, it was the word, the "rightly" spoken human word that I received into myself, in the most real sense. Speech here first, in this world of fiction as fiction, won its adequacy; certainly it appeared heightened, but heightened to itself. It was only a matter of time, however, until—as always happened—someone fell for a while into recitation, a "noble" recitation. Then, along with the genuine spokenness of speech, dialogical speech or even monological (in so far as the monologue was just an addressing of one's own person as a fellow man and no recitation), this whole world, mysteriously built out of the surprise and law, was shattered for me—until after some moments it arose anew with the return of the over-against. Since then it has sometimes come to pass, in the midst of the casualness of the everyday, that while I was sitting in the garden of an inn in the countryside of Vienna, a conversation penetrated to me from a neighboring table (perhaps an argument over falling prices by two market wives taking a rest), in which I perceived the spokenness of speech, sound becoming "Each-Other." [11]

When Buber begins with himself, he begins, in fact, with the spoken word. Notice that the university seminars opened for him the "free intercourse between teacher and students" as they interpreted texts together. But what affected Buber the most was the theater with its "rightly spoken human word." In the context of the theater, dialogical speech appeared heightened. The genuine spokenness of dialogue entered him and, after departing, he "arose anew with the return of the over-against." Through the direct address of speech, Buber discovered the other; discovering the other, Buber recognized himself.

CLOSING TALE

Buber closes this talk by retelling an old jest, which was itself retold by a Zaddik.

There once was a man who was very stupid. When he got up in the morning it was so hard for him to find his clothes that at night he hesitated to go to bed for thinking of the trouble he would have on waking. One evening he finally made a great effort, took paper and pencil and as he undressed, noted down exactly where he had put everything he had on. The next morning, very well pleased with himself, he took the slip of paper in is hand and read: 'cap'—there it was, he set it on his head; 'pants'—there they lay, he got into them; and so it went until he was fully dressed. 'That's all very well, but now where am I myself?' he asked in great consternation. 'Where in the world am I?' He looked and looked, but it was a vain search; he could not find himself. 'And that is how it is with us,' said the Rabbi. (159)

This concluding tale offers a perfect segue to Buber's fifth talk. The conflict within the person who is not able to find the "self" for which he or she is searching is a warning to all those searching for God. The hero of this tale is a "man who was very stupid." The word "stupid" can suggest many things from lacking intelligence all the way to the Hindu teaching of *avidya*, beginningless ignorance. We are all stupid. When we try to help ourselves out of our predicament (i.e., by remembering our clothes), we still cannot find ourselves (i.e., the one who is trying to end his/her predicament). "And that," the Rabbi said, "is how it is with us." Just as we cannot see ourselves, the seeker (you/I) cannot finally be found by the one who seeks.

In the story, the stupid man was initially tempted to overcome his problem by not sleeping. His solution took both courage and creativity—the courage to break out of habitual inaction and to risk failure to effect change, and the creativity to envision a practical way to address his problem with the common sense method of simply writing a list to which he could refer in the morning. For these reasons, he was "very well pleased with himself." No sooner does he succeed in overcoming his problem by getting fully dressed to face the world then a far greater problem appears. Immediately upon dressing himself to face the world, he withdraws into thinking about where he himself stands: Here are my clothes, but where am I? Although he searched and pondered the problem, he could not find himself. This conundrum remains prevalent with spiritual seekers. We know what rituals and practices to use, but the temptation to withdraw from engaging in the stream of life into one's own thoughts about who one is—and to remain there—only reinforces the problem.

A similar dilemma is prevalent in many spiritual traditions form Sufism to Zen, from Native American religion to Pagan wisdom: The self who searches cannot find the self who searches for itself. My former teacher of Rinzai Zen used to call this conundrum "being trapped in dualistic consciousness." The subjective I who searches for itself as an object will be perpetually frustrated by the illusion that there is someone searching for a separate thing called the Self. "And that is how it is with us," said the Rabbi. This problem is not unique to any one of us. It is universal to all those who seek. For this reason, Buber suggests that to be fully responsible to yourself, it is necessary to find yourself in relationship to others, to the world, and to God. When Buber writes "everything depends on myself" and I must "straighten myself out," he is speaking of an inner intention (*kavana*) to enter into authentic relationships with the world. In all genuine engagements with others, I am given to recognize myself as an ever-unique dialogical person. It will become apparent why this tale perfectly bridges this talk to the next as Buber addresses this problem in his fifth seminar lecture.

PRACTICE EXERCISES

I. Chapter-Specific Questions

(Designed to bring greater clarity to Buber's central insights.)

1. What is most needed if you are to have a unified soul, that is, "straighten yourself out?" Put another way, how can you find your way from the "casual, accessory elements of existence to your own self?" What is it that prevents you from the straightening? And how can this be overcome?
2. Buber says that the origin of all conflict stems from the fact that "I do not say what I mean, and that I do not do what I say." Is it possible to avoid conflict-situations? How do *you* avoid conflict situations? How do you respond to this? Do you agree or disagree with Buber? Why?
3. When Rabbi Hanokh responds to the "stupid" man's not being able to find himself—"that's how it is with us"—what is he implying first, about the stupid man, and second, about you? Where do you look to find yourself?
4. Give an example in which you say what you mean and do what you say. How did it make your life easier?

II. Comparative Questions

(Designed to deepen your dialogue with Buber's spiritual practices.)

1. Now and then a question addresses you with some urgency but does not need an immediate answer. Looking back at these specific questions, select one that would be helpful to live with without yet having a clear answer. Are you willing to live within the question, so to speak, and allow its echoes, its implications, and its edges to affect the way you relate to the world? What happens to that question when you bring it, unanswered, into your dialogue with others? When is the right time to return to the question and allow an answer to form itself for you?

2. What is the key element of this talk, the central insight upon which the entire presentation is based? How does it challenge you? Imagine yourself in a conversation with Buber about one of these questions that most challenges you or most surprises you. What do you think Buber would say? In response, what would you say to Buber?
3. Following Buber's interpretation of the Hasidic tradition in this presentation, what practice could you initiate, or intensify, in your life that would embody this understanding? What is the first thing you would do? Then what?
4. What does the dynamic relation between Rabbi Yitzhak and Rabbi David of Lelov suggest about the path we need to take? With whom do you most identify in this story? How would you have acted either similarly or differently than either of these teachers?

III. Feedback Questions

(Designed to help you achieve life-integrations in meaningful dialogue with others.)

1. Select a question from the first two sections that deeply grasped you to bring into dialogue with someone else who has also read Buber's talks. After engaging that question in dialogue with another person, what new insights/understandings emerged from the dialogical interaction itself?
2. Formulate your own question about the meaning and/or practice of Buber's teaching; bring it into dialogue with another person and record the results. What did you come to realize as a result of that dialogue?
3. Of all the correlations between various responses you have made in your Journal, which one is of greatest value? How have you integrated it into your daily life?
4. Create a dialogue script with Buber in which you ask a heart-felt question and then listen to hear Buber's response as if it is aimed uniquely at you. In this script, ask a question and, before answering, listen quietly to allow what Buber might say to form itself in your mind. Later, you may wish to share your dialogue script with friends or family. Notice how subsequent dialogical relationships are charged.

Chapter 5

Turning toward Others

"Turning is capable of renewing a [person] *from within and changing* [one's] *position in God's world, so that* [one] *who turns is seen standing above the perfect* zaddik [fulfilled teacher], *who does not know the abyss of sin."* (163)

SUMMARY OF BUBER'S FIFTH TALK

Buber's fifth talk, "Not to be Preoccupied with Oneself," seems almost contradictory at first glance to the immediately preceding talk. Buber begins this talk by telling how one Rabbi confided in another Rabbi that he was heartsick with worry because his hair and beard had grown white and because he had not yet atoned. In response, Rabbi Eliezer told him to forget about himself and think of the world. The goal of life does not lie in preoccupation with self, but with an active relationship with the world, with bringing our gifts and abilities to the community. The central teaching of this story, therefore, is accomplishing what the white-haired, white-bearded Rabbi had failed to perform—namely, true turning. More important than pursuing one's own salvation, much greater than acts of penance, *turning* away from self-preoccupations, and towards others, the world, and God is central to Jewish teaching of the human way. Turning is a two-way movement: a reversal of one's whole being away from the isolating maze of selfishness, self-intending, and self-absorption and toward others, toward the world, toward relationships. Practicing genuine turning, from self-orientation toward the otherness of the other, for Buber both renews you from within and deepens your relationship with God in the world.

OPENING HASIDIC TALE

Buber begins the fifth talk, once again, by quoting a Hasidic tale about one Rabbi giving advice to another:

> *Rabbi Hayyim of Zans* [in Western Galicia] *had married his son to the daughter of Rabbi Eliezer. The day after the wedding he visited the father of the bride and said: 'Now that we are related I feel close to you and can tell you what is eating at my heart. Look! My hair and beard have grown white, and I have not yet atoned!'*
> *'O my friend,' replied Rabbi Eliezer, 'you are thinking only of yourself. How about forgetting yourself and thinking of the world?'* (162)

KEY TEACHINGS AND PRACTICES

In this brief tale, we hear about Rabbi Hayyim's anxiety, which has been triggered by his growing older. His fears are not about what the poet T. S. Eliot described in his poem *Four Quartets* as "the cold friction of expiring sense," or the recognition in old age of "human folly" and "laughter at what ceases to amuse," or "the rending pain or re-enactment of all that you have done, and been." Rabbi Hayyim is troubled, instead, about appearances, both physical and spiritual. He is troubled because his hair and beard have grown white before he has atoned, or truly turned toward dialogue. In a simple yet profound response, Rabbi Eliezer replied, "How about forgetting yourself and thinking of the world?" Though this advice seems to contradict everything Buber has said up to this point about the importance of preparing oneself, beginning with oneself does not mean ending with oneself or becoming preoccupied with oneself. Rather than worrying in a spirit of self-reproach about our wrongdoings, we are called to use our energy and efforts to activate our relationships with the world.

But why, in this tale, is Rabbi Hayyim's concern about atonement, usually regarded as an integral part of faith and religion, presented as being self-involved? Atonement itself is not the problem in this story. Atonement only becomes problematic when it involves self-torture or a desire to repent primarily for one's own sake. Atonement can best be accomplished through selfless engagement. In his interpretation of this story, it appears to Buber that Rabbi Hayyim has begun to turn but has stopped part way, and so he is being urged by Eliezer to continue to turn, to turn completely.

Guilt entrenches us in feelings of selfish inadequacy where we are conscious of all we have not done in comparison with all that has been done by others. As a result, we feel as though we should follow the examples set forth by others because we feel incomplete and are blinded from our true self and from seeing our unique "particular way." Guilt and repentance require an enormous amount of energy. Think about how taxing it is to beat yourself up! Instead of using your energy to "move forward in the world," you are using it to wallow in yourself.

NOT AIMING AT YOURSELF

We can come to understand Buber's meaning better here by placing his words against the backdrop of their opposite—the irrational, unreal, internalized "I." In his essay "On the Psychologizing of the World," Buber speaks of our fundamental problem: that we insist on seeing the world through a psychological filter of judgments and assessments. That is,

> *Psychologizing of the world is the inclusion of the world in the soul, the transference of the world into the soul, but not just any such transference but only that which goes so far that the essential is thereby disturbed . . . This essential is the facing of I and world. That the world faces me and that between us the real happens, this essential basic relation from which our life receives its meaning is injured if the world is so far removed within the soul that its non-pyschic reality is obliterated, that this fundamental relation of I to world ceases to be able to be a relation of I to Thou.*[1]

Signs of our addiction to the internalizing or "psychologizing" process Buber is describing here abound. Consider, for example, the many books, workshops, and therapies aimed at the self. Think of the self-realization spiritual movements that invite you to awaken to true self. A poster at a local bookstore reads:

> **Who Am I?**
> An
> Opportunity to
> Gently and deeply
> Explore yourself,
> Your views, and
> What lies
> Beyond.
> Retreat focused on
> Self-Knowledge
> Through clear
> Insight and
> Profound
> Understanding.

The use of terms such as "self-actualization," "self-realization," and "realizing your potentialities" have become popular mantras in our culture. But by internalizing everything in this way, we actually move away from potential wholeness and only reinforce the "I" side of our human relationships.

These psychologizing approaches to living are especially problematic because they do not address a fundamental question: if I already am myself, what is it that I need to realize? If I am not already the person I hope to become, whatever I do to become that person won't add or subtract from who I am. Furthermore, if I am fated to become what I hope to become because the universe wants to manifest my "true self" to me, then I need not do much of anything to achieve it except to become aware of my spiritual nature.

According to Buber, we do not control our own destinies, we are not fated to manifest our inner spirit, and we do not "actualize" ourselves. Instead, we become ourselves only when we meet others spontaneously. When left to itself without any contact with a Thou, the world of the individual becomes estranged and isolated. As long as I remain tucked away securely in my own self-consciousness, no matter how heightened that self-consciousness may seem, I will continue to live outside of genuine relationship.

Referring back to his last talk and ahead to what he is about to say, Buber says,

> One need only ask one question: 'What for?' What am I to choose my particular way for? What am I to unify my being for? The reply is: Not for my own sake. This is why the previous injunction was: to begin with oneself, but not to end with oneself; to start from oneself, but not to aim at oneself; to comprehend oneself, but not to be preoccupied with oneself. (162)

Although difficult, it is necessary to begin with yourself but not to remain focused on yourself. Instead, it is crucial to apply the wasted energy of the pursuit of self-attainment toward active relationship with the world. It is for this reason that Rabbi Eliezer says, "Be preoccupied with the world not with yourself." But how is this to be accomplished?

TURNING

In his comments on this tale, Buber points out that Rabbi Hayyim has not yet "performed the true turning" to the world, to others, or to God. That the Rabbi is worried about how he looks, about the whiteness in his hair and beard, prompts Rabbi Eliezer's response. Rabbi Hayyim is busy looking into his individualizing, self-absorbed thoughts, which in turn reinforces his sense of despondency. As long as he is more worried about how he appears to others, about his age and his not having atoned, than about genuine relationship, he never will be redeemed. It is as if someone has told you, in response to the complaint "I'm lonely" or "I'm unloved," "Well, then, go out and find someone in need of your attention" or "Go befriend someone." By turning to the world your truest self emerges. By reversing your attention from yourself to others, you open yourself to relational grace.[2]

The practice of "turning" is central to Hasidic spiritual teaching. Failure to turn whole-heartedly toward the other traps us in our individuality, in a one-sided relation to the world. For Buber, turning with one's whole being toward others is capable of renewing a person from within. First, Buber says

> we should properly understand what is said here about turning. It is known that turning stands in the center of the Jewish conception of the [human way]. Turning is capable of renewing a [person] from within and changing [his or her] position in God's world, so that [he or she] who turns is seen standing above the perfect zaddik, who does not know the abyss of sin. (164)

This is a unique, even radical, insight into the human condition. When we genuinely turn away from the separated self-will, from merely experiencing and using everything, whether people or information, toward encountering, mutually accepting, affirming, and confirming others, we can come to glimpse this moment's God. Interhuman spirituality is, therefore, a spirituality of reciprocal "betweenness," something that emerges in relation between person and person. Its method, or practice, is real dialogue; its result is mutual transformation.

Buber follows this enticing idea with one that points toward what prevents us from true turning. Referring to the person who withholds energy from the practice of direct and mutual address in the world, Buber quotes the Rabbi of Ger:

> 'He who has done ill and talks about it and thinks about it all the time does not cast the base thing he did out of his thoughts, and whatever one thinks, therein one is, one's soul is wholly and utterly in what one thinks, and so he dwells in baseness. He will certainly not be able to turn, for his spirit will grow coarse and his heart stubborn. . . . (165)

Rabbi Hayyim finds himself, like many of us, "dwelling in the baseness" of contemplating our personal failures to the exclusion of real relationship.

A DOUBLE MOVEMENT

After a seminar at San Jose State University on Buber's *I and Thou*, one afternoon a young instructor from the philosophy department (who had been attending the seminar) asked a question that significantly challenged the context of the seminar: "What does Buber say about how I should enter into relationships? Should I prepare for dialogue in a certain way?" In other words, can one do something before entering dialogue? We can say that Buber would have answered directly that one cannot prepare for "genuine dialogue" except by fostering a willingness to turn.

There are two basic directions of movement, according to Buber, that any one of us can make at any moment in response to a situation. The first direction of movement he calls "reflexion," or bending back on oneself. This backward-bending movement elevates self-consciousness and leads to withdrawal from relationships with others. It allows the other to exist only within the content of my own experience. As a consequence, when we get stuck in self-reflection, the heart and soul of what is most human gets lost. This happens each time I "turn away" from the other who encounters me or calls me forth into the world.

The other basic movement he calls "turning towards." It refers to turning from self-absorption and toward genuine dialogue with another, and it happens through both personal will and relational grace. Our willed effort to turn away from anything that prevents us from entering into genuine relationship with the other is essential. At the same time, relational grace— the spirit of the "between"—is requisite. Without it, genuine dialogue is impossible. For Buber, the act of "turning" streams through all of the spheres of existence and renews the world. Toward whom do you turn most easily?

"Turning" requires a double movement of the soul. First, we must learn to turn *away from* everything that would prevent us from entering into genuine relationship with the other; and second, we must turn *toward* whomever or whatever presents itself to us:

Table 5.1.

From Separation	Toward Deep Bonding
Self-Asserting Instincts	With the World
Self-Serving Individuality	With Others
Selfish Forms of Solitude	With the Primal Source

As we turn away from self-preoccupation, we must also be careful to turn toward genuine relationship and not toward another *I-It* object.

We all experience resistance to this idea. I can always conjure up apparently good reasons for *not* turning. "I am working on myself," or "The people in my life must turn toward me first" are two of the most common. They assume that the time for genuine dialogue is later, after the "I" has been appeased. As difficult as it might seem to turn away from oneself and toward others, however, it only takes one act, one shift of habitual thinking, one reversal of the norm: it requires becoming open to the unlimited possibilities emerging from relationship. It requires not having a particular object, goal, or desire in mind when we encounter the other. Each time we engage that one act of turning without an agenda, it becomes incrementally easier to continue doing so.

MR. M.

By 1910 or 1911 Buber realized his "inborn binding with Hasidic truth." Buber had recently completed *The Tales of Rabbi Nachman* (1906) and *The Legend of the Baal-Shem* (1907). At the time Buber felt that he bore in himself "the blood and the spirit of those who created [Hasidic legends], and out of my blood and spirit it has become new."[3] The Hasidic teaching which continued to draw Buber is based on an existential trust that

> *no thing can exist without a divine spark, and each person can uncover and redeem this spark at each time and through each action, even the most ordinary, if only* [he or she] *performs it in purity, wholly directed to God and concentrated in Him.*[4]

Hasidism, therefore, took the social form of small, popular communities whose aim was preserving God's love for everyone, indeed for all things.

Once after his lecture (it was the third in a series of talks on Judaism), Buber went to a coffee house with several members of the association who arranged the evening lecture. While discussing a theme of moral philosophy, a middle-aged Jewish man came to their table. In response to Buber's somewhat distant greeting, the man replied with a slight reproof: "Doctor! Do you not recognize me?" No doubt engrossed in the significant ideas of the conversation, Buber was caught off guard. Initially, he was less than fully present.

When Buber answered in the negative, the man introduced himself as M., the brother of a former steward of Buber's father. Buber immediately invited Mr. M. to sit with the group and inquired about circumstances in his life. When the group gathered at the table returned to the conversation at hand,

Mr. M. listened with eager attentiveness. Yet it was obvious to Buber that he did not understand a single word.

After a while Buber asked Mr. M. whether he perhaps had something to say to Buber and that if he did he would gladly go to one side with him to talk about his concern. However Mr. M. vigorously declined and the conversation at the table started up again with Mr. M. listening. When a half hour or more had passed, Buber again inquired whether he wished to ask Buber anything. Then, in the wake of Buber's turning his full attention to Mr. M., they fell into an honest exchange. This time, Mr. M. said very timidly: "Doctor, I should like to ask you a question."

"Just ask, Mr. M.," Buber encouraged him. "I shall gladly give you information as best I can."

"Doctor," M. said, "I have a daughter. And I also have a young man for my daughter. He is a student of law. He passed the examinations with distinction." Here he paused. Buber looked at him encouragingly, supposing that the man wished to entreat Buber to use his influence in some way on behalf of the presumptive son-in-law.

"Doctor," he asked, "is he a steady man?"

Buber was surprised but felt that he should not refuse to answer. "Now, Mr. M.," Buber explained, "after what you have said it can certainly be taken for granted that he is industrious and able."

Still he questioned further. "But Doctor," he said, "does he also have a good head?"

"That is even more difficult to answer," Buber replied, "but at any rate he has not succeeded with industry alone, he must also have something in his head."

Once again Mr. M. paused. Then he asked, clearly as a final question: "Doctor, should he now become a judge or a lawyer?"

"About that I can give you no information," Buber answered. "I do not know the young man, indeed, and even if I did know him, I should hardly be able to advise in this matter."

Then Mr. M., looking almost melancholy, half-complaining, half-understanding, spoke in an indescribable tone, composed in equal part of sorrow and humility: "Doctor, you do not *want* to say—now, I thank you for what you have said to me."

Calling the encounter that followed with Mr. M. a "humorous and meaningful occurrence, which apparently has nothing to do with Hasidism," Buber indicated that the incident afforded him, nonetheless, "a new and significant insight into it." And what was that? Buber reflects that as a child he had received the image of the zaddik as "pure idea, the idea of the genuine leader of a genuine community." Then, between his youth and growth into adulthood this idea developed into that of "the perfected man who realizes God in the world." But now, Buber remarks, in light of this event:

> *I caught sight in my inner experience of the zaddik's function as a leader. I, who am truly no zaddik, no one assured in God, rather a man endangered before God, a man wrestling ever anew for God's light, ever anew engulfed in God's abysses, nonetheless, when asked a trivial question and replying with a trivial answer, then experienced from within for the first time the true zaddik, questioned about revelations and replying in revelations. I experienced him in the fundamental relation of his soul to the world: in his responsibility.*[5]

REDIRECTING YOUR SOUL POWER

During a conversation about Buber's Hasidic teaching, a friend who had read *The Way of Man* and who had recently heard me speak about Buber's Hasidic spirituality in a Catholic church remarked with great frustration: "Okay, I know what Buber is saying, but I don't know how to do it. The demands of the world keep intervening in my life. I get too busy. I forget. I get distracted. How can I practice it?"

This is exactly the frustration that Rabbi Eliezer addresses in a very general sense when he says, "Do not keep worrying about what you have done wrong, but apply the soul power you are now wasting on self-reproach, to such active relationship to the world as you are destined for. You should not be occupied with yourself but with the world" (164)

Can you imagine what this might be like? Why do you think Buber made such a point of this?

To be fair to Buber's emphasis, why not place your responses to these questions next to his. Buber instructs us not to be preoccupied with ourselves, and I would add that this applies even to our answers to these questions, no matter how justifiable or valid our answers seem. Buber's point is simple: stop wasting all the energy that you use to justify yourself or legitimize your own position. Instead, redirect that energy, that passion, toward making a difference in the world.

I can hear Buber encouraging us to take all the effort we use to fret and worry, to complain and express our anxieties, and to instead apply that effort toward doing something positive in the world. Worrying about what you haven't been able to accomplish for whatever reason only ties you down to the past. Why not, instead, start fresh, right now? Start by transforming the passion that you use for making excuses into helping someone else, or serving someone, or bringing a good project to completion.

Try it. See what happens. See if, as Buber remarks, turning in this way renews you from within and changes your position in God's world. What is there to lose?

TRANSPARENT TO THE ABSOLUTE

Every act of genuine turning eventually leads one to the presence of God. In Buber's words,

> *Turning is capable of renewing a* [person] *from within and changing his* [or her] *position in God's world . . . but turning means here something much greater than repentance and acts of penance; it means that by a reversal of* [one's] *whole being, a* [person] *who had been lost in the maze of selfishness . . . finds a way to God, that is, a way to the fulfillment of the particular task for which . . . this particular* [person], *has been destined by God.* (163)

Buber's point here can be stated this way: when a person truly turns toward the other and responds with real responsibility, when we turn toward the other with sense of the other's thoughts, feelings, and experiences, the relationship becomes "transparent into the absolute." Like music, our life begins to "assume the cadence of an inwardness" that stirs one's "heart of hearts." The divine voice, according to Buber, addresses us not as isolated individuals, but as relational persons in and through interhuman *immediacy*. For immediacy to happen, though, we must learn to listen attentively to the other, to attune ourselves to the heartstrings of the divinely spoken word manifest in all our relations.

For Buber, this relational life cannot be understood intellectually. The ground and meaning of Buber's foundational principle, his philosophy of the *interhuman*, is not a position that stands over and against other positions, or an experience to be recorded as the content of one's consciousness, or an idea to be compared to others. Rather, the interhuman refers to a living reality that (1) calls for *interaction* (authentic dialogue) and (2) points to a *place* (the between) that emerges between I and Thou when we practice the sacramental act of genuine turning.

SACRAMENTAL EXISTENCE

If Buber is right, Hasidic spirituality is a series of God-infused moments of sacramental existence, of God-infused decisions to turn away from oneself and toward the world. That is, the practice of turning revitalizes the first and foremost teaching of Hasidic spirituality: that God needs us to fulfill God's presence in the world. In fact, Hasidic revelation, and biblical revelation before it, insist on an absolute distinction between God and us. We are not part and parcel of God, the content of God's thoughts, or players in some predetermined plan. If no distinction between God and us existed, there would be no possibility of dialogue between us and God. God *appears* and *speaks* as a separate Person when we turn wholly Godward. This applies to those we meet.

A complete act of turning demands a shift in the direction of one's attention and a complete reversal away from whatever it is that keeps us locked in a cycle of monologue. Turning, when one makes a serious effort to do so, is both a preliminary behavior and a permanent act. The significance of the Hasidic tale, Buber says, goes beyond this, though. Whenever we focus on our deeds or misdeeds, we remain trapped within the context of our own experiences. Indeed, this is one of the main points on which Christianity differs from Judaism.

> [Christianity] *makes each* [person's] *salvation his* [or her] *highest aim. Judaism regards each* [person's] *soul as a serving member of God's Creation which, by* [his or her] *work, is to become the Kingdom of God; thus no soul has its object in itself, in its own salvation.* (165)

For this reason, the pursuit of one's own salvation is considered, in Hasidic Judaism, merely as the "sublimest form of self-intending." While it is true that we should try to purify ourselves, this purification should not be undertaken for the sake of eternal bliss or "salvation," but for the sake of the real work that we want to perform in the world.

REDEMPTION

Buber concludes his classic *I and Thou* with a provocative remark: "But the event that from the side of the world is called turning is called from God's side redemption."[6] Redemption involves an ever-renewed willingness to risk one's individuality by turning toward the presence of the other and entering into the deep bond of interhuman relationships. Truly redemptive turning, Buber indicates in *I and Thou,* means turning both toward the other (whomever or whatever we meet) and toward the relational bond between you and the other.

In contrast to self-reflexive behaviors that do little to urge us toward the life of dialogue, Buber stresses the need for us to turn toward a deep bonding with others. We should, in other words, turn toward "connection," and it is only by turning toward connection that we truly expand into our own beings:

*For the two primary metacosmical movements of the world—expansion into
its own being and turning to connection—find their supreme human form, the
real spiritual form of their struggle and adjustment, their mingling and separation, in the history of the human relation to God. In turning the Word is born
on earth, in expansion the Word enters the chrysalis form of religion, in fresh
turning it is born again with new wings.[7]*

Here Buber indicates the necessity of turning toward relationship itself,
toward binding and healing togetherness, in order for the Word to take flight
in the world.

The full human way is the path on which we choose again and again to go
forth into the possibility of deep bonding. The human way, which gives voice
to God in the world, requires "turning" without holding oneself back, turning
with one's whole existence toward who or what is with us. From within our
experience of monologue and division, an impulse emerges that enables us
to re-enter the world. Redemption from the human side, both personal and
historical, involves an ever-renewed willingness, or openness, to risk one's
individuality in the presence of relationship.

The realization of God's manifestation (*theophany*) is glimpsed in the
sphere that lies between beings. This sphere of the between, which Buber
calls the Kingdom of God, often "hides in our midst," waiting to be disclosed
to us. Disclosure of the Kingdom of God between person and person as we
turn toward the other is true redemption, and, as we have seen, it does not
simply depend upon God. Each of us helps to bring about and to renew the
unity of God and the world through genuine relationship. Redemption manifests in our discovering the common *humanness* in our midst.

This is why, for Buber, echoing Rabbi Bunam, no soul has as its object
its own salvation. The road to redemption involves a history of two kinds of
people: the proud and the humble.

Rabbi Bunam thus sees, as it were, the history of [humankind] *on its road to
redemption as a process involving two kinds of* [persons], *the proud who, if
sometimes in the sublimest form, think of themselves, and the humble, who in all
matters think of the world. Only when pride subjects itself to humility can it be
redeemed; and only when it is redeemed, can the world be redeemed.* (166)

After Rabbi Bunam died, one of his disciples remarked,

*'Rabbi Bunam had the keys to all the firmaments. And why not? A man who does
not think of himself is given all the keys.'* (166–7)

The reason, according to Buber, that Rabbi Bunam was given the keys to all
the firmaments at his death was because during his life he did not think of

himself. Only when pride subjects itself to humility is redemption possible. Indeed, to enter the life of dialogue, humility is necessary. Humility, as T. S. Eliot wrote, "is endless." So too is the redemptive practice turning toward dialogue.

BUBER LIFE ANECDOTE

In previous chapters, we have seen that Buber's life concretely exemplifies his spirituality. The following anecdote illustrates the main theme of this talk—"turning"—in relation to Buber's early inability to practice it and his subsequent realization of its necessity. Until his mid-thirties, Buber saw his spiritual life as marked by moments of mystical ecstasy during which he was lifted out of the ordinary. As World War I was breaking out, in July 1914, a young man came to visit Buber after Buber had experienced a morning of ecstatic reverie in mediation and prayer. The young man and Buber conversed attentively, but Buber, by his own admission, failed to turn to him completely, failed to hear the young man's deeper concerns that lay beneath the surface of their conversation. Later, learning that the young man was killed at the front in the war, Buber confessed:

> *Since then I have given up the "religious," which is nothing but the exception, extraction, exaltation, ecstasy; or it has given me up. I possess nothing but the everyday out of which I am never taken. The mystery is no longer disclosed, it has escaped or it has made its dwelling here where everything happens where it happens. I know no fullness but each mortal hour's fullness of claim and responsibility. Though far from being equal to it, yet I know that in the claim I am claimed and may respond in responsibility, and know who speaks and demands a response.*

Although the young man and Buber in this story conversed attentively, Buber failed to turn to him completely. In other words, he failed to grasp whatever fundamental life-question the student did not ask directly. Buber failed to hear or notice the young man's deeper concerns that remained beneath the surface of speech. Buber had not been fully attentive or fully present. Nor had he listened obediently. Buber came to realize that "genuine dialogue"—direct, honest, open, spontaneous, mutual, address-response communication in the midst of the every day—and not religious reverie is at the center of the soul's search for God:

> *I do not know much more. If that is religion then it is just everything, simply all that is lived in its possibility of dialogue. Here is space also for religion's*

*highest forms. As when you pray you do not thereby remove yourself from this
life of yours but in your praying refer your thought to it, even though it may
be in order to yield it; so too in the unprecedented and surprising, when you
are called upon from above, required, chosen, empowered, sent, you with this
your mortal bit of life are meant. This moment is not extracted from it, it rests
on what has been and beckons to the remainder that has still to be lived. You
are not swallowed up in a fullness without obligation, you are willed for the
life of communion*[8]

When Buber was 75, a young man asked him how he discovered the gift of
understanding in himself. After a pause, Buber answered:

*It came to me through a devastating experience during World War I, when I was
in my late thirties. A young man came to see me, as you have come to see me.
We sat talking as we are now. But I failed him. And this forced me to ask myself,
why did you fail him? I have written about this, and how it caused a decisive
change in my thinking which has remained until today.*[9]

Too often when we are wrapped in self-directed "religious enthusiasm,"
genuine meeting cannot occur. Had Buber fully opened himself to the address
of the young man—presence-to-presence in the moment of meeting—the
despair of death that Buber only later sensed beneath the man's words might
have been disclosed. As a result, Buber concluded that special moments of
private religious experience only impede our genuine relationship to God.
Buber thought of this grave mismeeting not only as a judgment on his whole
way of life, but also as the foundation for his recognition of the life of dialogue. What catalyzed Buber's realization that dialogue is at the heart of
Hasidism was his understanding, too late, that he had *failed* to turn wholly
toward the young student and, simultaneously, failed to open himself up to a
genuine relationship with God. As a result, the young man died of a despair
that did not oppose his own death.

CLOSING TALE

As he does in his other talks, Buber concludes his fifth with another Hasidic
tale, but this time he adds his own elaboration. In this tale,

*The greatest of Rabbi Bunam's disciples, a truly tragic figure among the zad-
dikim, Rabbi Mendel of Kotzk, once said to his congregation: 'What, after all,
do I demand of you? Only three things: not to look furtively outside yourselves,
not to look furtively into others, and not to aim at yourselves.'* (167)

Buber then continues

> *That is to say: firstly, everyone should preserve and hallow his own soul in its*
> *own particularity and in its own place, and not envy the particularity and place*
> *of others; secondly, everyone should respect the secret in the soul of his fellow-*
> *man, and not, with brazen curiosity, intrude upon it and take advantage of it;*
> *and thirdly, everyone, in his relationship to the world, should be careful not to*
> *set himself as his aim.* (167)

Buber's comment on Rabbi Mandel of Kotzk reveals most clearly the necessary relation between his fourth and fifth talks. Although you must start with yourself, all is lost if you continue aiming at yourself. Just as it is necessary to hallow your own unique soul, in all its particularity, it is equally necessary to hallow the soul of your friends and family, of all those toward whom you turn.

Hasidism offers a way of redemption to everyone at every stage of life. This redemption is called "turning." Even when we lose our way, turn away from our origins or run directionless, we are able to turn again if we become conscious of self-preoccupation, stop hiding, take responsibility for ourselves and affirm ourselves in God's presence. The person who turns away from directionlessness and towards God with his or her whole self releases the divine immanence (his/her divine spark) from the shell of individuality into the world.

PRACTICE EXERCISES

I. Chapter-Specific Questions

(Designed to bring greater clarity to Buber's central insights.)

1. What happens to you when you are thinking only of yourself? What happens to you when you think of another? Describe the shift from the former to the latter.
2. Is Rabbi Mendel's advice—"to hallow your own soul" and "not to aim at yourself"—contradictory? Can each of these statements be true in your life? If so, how?
3. How does the practice of "turning" (away from self-interest toward the otherness of the other) renew you from within? To whom do you turn most easily?
4. List ways in which self-preoccupation prevents you from turning toward God. Which of these would be the most difficult to overcome? Which, the easiest?

II. Comparative Questions

(Designed to deepen your dialogue with Buber's spiritual practices.)

1. Now and then a question addresses you with a unique urgency without needing an immediate answer. Looking back at these specific questions, select one that would be helpful to live with without your yet having a clear answer. Are you willing to live within the question, so to speak, and allow its echoes, its implications, and its edges to affect the way you relate to the world? What happens to that question when you bring it, unanswered, into your discourse? When is the time right to return to the question and allow an answer to form itself for you?
2. What is the key element of this talk, the central insight upon which the entire presentation is based? How does it challenge you? Imagine yourself in a conversation with Buber about one of the questions that most challenges you or which most surprises you. Considering the context of his fifth talk, what do you think Buber would say? In response, what would you say to Buber?
3. Following Buber's interpretation of the Hasidic tradition in this presentation, what practice could you initiate, or intensify, in your life that would embody this understanding? What is the first thing you would do? Then what?
4. What does the dynamic relation between rebbe and disciple indicate about the disciple's behavior? With whom do you most identify in this story? How would you have acted either similarly or differently from the disciple?

III. Feedback Questions

(Designed to help you achieve life-integrations in meaningful dialogue with others.)

1. Select a question from the first two sections that deeply grasped you to bring into dialogue with someone else who has also read Buber's talks. After engaging that question in dialogue with another person, what new insights/understandings emerged from the dialogue itself?
2. Formulate your own question about the meaning and/or practice of Buber's teaching; bring it into dialogue with someone else and record the results. What did you come to realize as a result of that dialogue?
3. Of all the correlations between various responses you have made in your Journal, which one is of greatest value? How have you integrated it into your daily life?

4. Create a dialogue script with Buber in which you ask your heartfelt question and then listen to hear Buber's response as if that response has been aimed uniquely at you. In this script, you ask a question, and then before answering, listen quietly to allow what Buber might say to form itself in your mind. Later, you may wish to share your dialogue script with friends or family. Notice how subsequent dialogical relationships are charged.

Chapter 6

Here Where You Stand

"This is the ultimate purpose: to let God in . . . where we really stand, where we live, where we live a true life." (176)

SUMMARY OF BUBER'S SIXTH TALK

The last of the six talks, "Here Where One Stands," begins with the tale of a Hasidic Jew being led in a dream to travel to a foreign place to find treasure. After arriving there, he is divinely inspired to find the treasure in his own home. The great treasure which Buber calls "the fulfillment of existence" can only be found in the place where one stands. That is, my essential task—fulfilling the human way—happens in the details of my daily life, in the specific environment where I am situated. This is your/our ultimate purpose—to let God into our life. By performing our daily tasks with "holy intent," we allow the light of the hidden divine life to shine. Two worlds that are often separated—the sacred, the ordinary—become one. In open and authentic relationship with others, therefore, God's intention for human fulfillment can be realized. "It is my conviction," Buber says, that by hallowing the world we not only open up a place for the Divine Presence to enter into it, but as well we become ourselves "humanly holy." The fulfillment of existence, discovering the ultimate purpose for which you were created—letting God into your life—occurs when you establish a dwelling place for the Divine Presence by maintaining holy interaction with the world right here and now where you are standing and where you live.

OPENING HASIDIC TALE

Buber begins his last presentation by retelling the Hasidic tale about a treasure buried under the stove in Rabbi Eizik's house.

> Rabbi Bunam used to tell young men who came to him for the first time the story of Rabbi Eizik, son of Rabbi Yekel of Cracow. After many years of great poverty which had never shaken his faith in God, he dreamed someone bade him look for a treasure in Prague, under the bridge which leads to the king's palace. When the dream recurred a third time, Rabbi Eizik prepared for the journey and set out for Prague. But the bridge was guarded day and night and he did not dare to start digging. Nevertheless he went to the bridge every morning and kept walking around it until evening. Finally the captain of the guards, who had been watching him, asked in a kindly way whether he was looking for something or waiting for somebody. Rabbi Eizik told him of the dream which had brought him here from a faraway country. The captain laughed: 'And so to please the dream, you poor fellow wore out your shoes to come here! As for having faith in dreams, if I had had it, I should have had to get going when a dream once told me to go to Cracow and dig for treasure under the stove in the room of a Jew—Eizik, son of Yekel, that was the name! Eizik, son of Yekel! I can just imagine what it would be like, how I should have to try every house over there, where one half of the Jews are named Eizik and the other Yekel!' And he laughed again. Rabbi Eizik bowed, travelled home, dug up the treasure from under the stove, and built the House of Prayer which is called 'Reb Eizik Reb Yekel's Shul.' 'Take this story to heart,' Rabbi Bunam used to add, 'and make what it says your own: There is something you cannot find anywhere in the world, not even at the zaddik's, and there is, nevertheless, a place where you can find it.' (170–71)

KEY TEACHINGS AND PRACTICES

Buber's last talk puts a crowning touch on his series of presentations. Buber's talks, as we have seen, move from God's question to Adam—"Where are you?"—in chapter 1, to the prerequisite spiritual practices of hallowing the everyday and unifying your soul, which then leads to practicing presentness by beginning with yourself and not taking yourself too seriously. This sixth talk points us very directly toward how we can answer God's initial call. The thesis of Buber's final talk, both radical and redemptive, concentrates our attention on the one thing necessary if we are to achieve our essential task in life, the humanly holy path: learning to find the sacred right where we stand. Buber speaks, in his concluding talk, of standing here and now in a dialogical partnership with God and the world, seeking to bring about God's kingdom on earth through service. Further, reflecting themes from former talks, Buber emphasizes that we should hallow not only our own souls and the souls of others, but our relationships as well.

The moral of the sixth Hasidic tale is that the fulfillment of existence is only possible in the environment that I feel to be natural, in the situation that has been assigned to me in the things that happen to me and claim me day after day. If we had power over the ends of the world and knew the secrets of the upper world, we would never experience that fulfillment of existence that a quiet, devoted relationship to nearby life can give us. The basis of Hasidic teaching, its core spirituality, is discovered here and now, under your own feet. In Buber's words,

> *There is something that can only be found in one place. It is a great treasure, which may be called the fulfillment of existence. The place where this treasure can be found is the place on which one stands. . . . for it is here where we stand that we should try to make shine the light of the hidden divine life.* (173)

"Here," for Buber, is nowhere other than the

> *environment which I feel to be the natural one, the situation which has been assigned to me as my fate, the things that happen to me day after day, the things that claim me day after day—these contain my essential task and such fulfillment of existence as is open to me.* (173)

Buber continues that it is "here, where we stand, that we should try to make shine the light of the hidden divine life." Even if we had power to travel to the ends of the earth, or to the upper worlds, it would not allow us to participate in true existence. This only happens when we perform "with holy intent, a task belonging to our daily duties" since "our treasure is hidden beneath the hearth of our own home."

LITTLE ENCOUNTERS

The phrase that Buber uses to describe the meetings that hold the potential to open us up to the presence of the immanent divine, "little encounters," encapsulates the central message of this talk and tale. In a potent remark, Buber underscores the Baal-Shem's teaching "that no encounter with a being or a thing in the course of our life lacks a hidden significance," which Buber calls "a mysterious spiritual substance." This mysterious substance is characterized by its dependence on us for helping it "towards its pure form." To the extent that we neglect developing genuine relationships with whom or what we encounter, we neglect this spiritual substance. Buber personalizes his address, in a way that he has not in any of the other talks, by stating, "it is my conviction that this [teaching] is essentially true." He then recasts the core of Hasidic teaching in his own words:

> *The highest culture of the soul remains basically arid and barren unless, day by day, waters of life pour forth into the soul from those little encounters to which we give their due; the most formidable power is intrinsically powerless unless it maintains a secret covenant with these contacts, both humble and helpful, with strange, and yet near, being.* (174)

The soul (body/mind/spirit) remains undernourished and parched unless waters of life pour forth into it. But from where? Precisely from our "little encounters," no matter how apparently insignificant, with persons, places, and things that continually cross our path. For spiritual health to flourish, it is necessary that these encounters become touchstones for us of a greater reality than what we are ordinarily used to.

Secret, yes, but by no means passive. Genuine relationship between persons is an unanticipated occurrence, a spontaneously reciprocal event. Rather than a self-contained "experience," the moment of meeting activates, between person and person, the emergence of something new that remains beyond words. For Buber, meeting in genuine dialogue activates an essential act of pure relationship in three dimensions: in the fullness of real mutuality, in the inexpressible confirmation of meaning, and in the fact that meaning is received in real life. In this sense, any encounter potentially opens us to meaning and a direction for our lives.

Can you think of ways to make this occur in your own life? Enacting and embodying a covenant between ourselves and the eternal partner, we enter whole-heartedly into relationship, both humbly and helpfully. God's relational presence, as a result of our effort, manifests itself in co-creative, co-revealing, co-redeeming ways. Our "I-focus" is replaced by "we-ness," the "it" is replaced by the "Thou." The dialogue itself has its own voice that, while seldom heard, shapes the way we engage with the other. In the energy of this spirit, our awareness of time and place temporarily disappear and we glimpse the presence of God. Here, spiritual health comes to fruition. For this reason, Buber says,

> *If we had power over the ends of the earth, it would not give us that fulfillment of existence which a quiet, devoted relationship to nearby life can give us. If we knew the secrets of the upper world, they would not allow us so much actual participation in true existence as we can achieve by performing with holy intent the task belonging to our daily duties.* (173)

It is "in the daily particulars of concrete living" that we find ourselves and achieve our potentiality. Here, home, the place where you stand: this is where your treasure lies. This is where we engage in relationship with one another. This is where we unify ourselves, release the divine spark, and let God in. When we hallow our relationships with each other here on earth, we create a place for God's participation in our lives. Thus, it is our "actual participation in true existence" that is holy and heavenly.

THE TREASURE

Rabbi Bunam's story about Eizik's dream of a treasure, about his search for "the fulfillment of existence," tells us that the fulfillment of our existence is to be found here where we have been set. But where exactly is this place? For Buber,

> *The environment which I feel to be the natural one, the situation which has been assigned to me as my fate, the things that happen to me day after day, the things that claim me day after day—these contain my essential task and such fulfillment of existence as is open to me.* (172)

Unfortunately, when things are not going well for us, our human tendency is to want to be somewhere else. "If I could only go there, then things would be different," we tell ourselves. True, the specifics of your situation would be different. But would *you* be any different? I once spent a summer in India making a spiritual pilgrimage to various ashrams and gurus, thinking that by going to such a holy place, it would make me holy. It didn't. Although exposed to sacred rituals, spiritual teachers, and holy teachers unlike anything I ever encountered, I experienced the same problems, anxieties, and suspicions in India that I did here.

Since no matter where I am I'm always here, we should ask ourselves how is it possible to discover the treasure that is right here where we stand. We can only do this by performing our tasks with "holy intent." The power of *kavana*, or "holy intent," is not found when we believe we have discovered the secrets of the upper world; rather, it is found in simply performing daily tasks with "right dedication." Acting out of a spirit of "right dedication" means responding with our whole being to the unique claim of each situation. Everything that we meet in life (animals, the earth, our tools, persons) contains "a mysterious spiritual substance [a divine spark] which depends on us for helping it towards its pure form, its perfection." Without developing genuine relationships, we neglect this spiritual substance and we are kept from living a fulfilled existence. Buber's conviction is that the soul remains barren unless it is watered, day by day, by those "little encounters" that maintain a covenant with the "strange, and yet near, being."

In contrast to religions which teach that this world is only appearance or illusion behind which lies the true world, Hasidism teaches that practicing holy intent in this world is (1) as important as it is in the world to come and (2) a link with the divine presence. Rather than positing two "separate and severed" worlds, Hasidic teaching tells us that in essence these become one through authentic dialogue. Our task is to work towards unifying these two worlds. This is why, if I had to choose just one of these talks to contemplate, one that captures the spirit of the others and also stands on its own as a consummating example of Hasidic spirituality, I would choose the sixth. In this talk, Buber's deepest Hasidic-oriented spirituality finds its fullest expression, particularly when he says,

> God's grace consists precisely in this, that he wants to let himself be won by [people], that he places himself, so to speak, into human hands. God wants to come to his world, but he wants to come to it through [people]. This is the mystery of our existence, the superhuman chance of humankind. (175)

Buber here offers a statement of his remarkable existential trust in God's unconditional love upon which Hasidic spiritual teachings are based. God shines through our concrete particularity, needing us to become trusting dialogical partners.

ANOTHER ASPECT

For Maurice Friedman, there is another essential aspect to this tale. Perhaps if Rabbi Eizik had not made his way to "Prague," Friedman suggests, he would never have discovered that the treasure was hidden beneath our own hearth. "There is meaning in our searching," he writes, "even when it takes us far afield, if it enables us to come back home to the unique task which awaits us. A young person raised in Judaism or Christianity is often barred from any genuine relationship to these religions by the fact that they are associated in his mind with the parents against whom he must rebel; with a social system the injustice of which is manifest; and often, in addition, with a shoddy way of presenting the religion that seems more concerned with group belonging or social snobbery than with anything genuinely religious. Such a person might find liberation in the teachings of Hinduism, Buddhism, or Zen Buddhism which he encounters unencumbered by relatives and institutions. After these have liberated him, he may be able to go back to find the treasure under his own hearth. When one does come back, it is with a new relationship such as only the fact of distancing makes possible."

Friedman continues, "This was my own experience in relation to Judaism. Brought up in a liberal Judaism of a very thin variety, I could never have returned to Judaism and established a new and deeper relationship with it had I not gone through Hinduism, Buddhism, Zen, Taoism, and Christian mysticism. Nor have I lost these other touchstones. They are part of the way in which I came to Hasidism and relate to it. Even if young people do not find their way back—and my own way to Hasidism was far more a way forward than a way back—they are still those who set out from Cracow. Whatever treasure they really find, however far it may be from home, is still bound to those original roots. These roots are embedded in the ground on which they stand and from which they respond to the new touchstones that call to them."[1] This search for fulfillment, according to Buber, is not a noun but a verb, not a thing but an action—"a quiet devoted relationship" to life.

STANDING

In order to understand the fullest implications for spiritual living in Buber's last talk, it is crucial to understand what Buber means by the word "stand." When Buber says "here where one stands," he is not referring to a fixed or permanent or inflexible position but rather to a dialogical openness in the present moment to whatever or whomever is encountered. In other words, your stand becomes a clearing, an opening for that for which you stand. Standing thus refers to a person's unique intellectual/emotive/spiritual stance or bearing from which you go forth to engage the world. Since we stand *in the world*, our stand always occurs in the presence of a dialogical partner, or nature, or art, or a film, or a text. There is no "real I" isolated by itself.

For Buber, there are two basic ways in which people find themselves within the world, one that Buber characterized the "I-Thou" *relationship* and the other the "I-It" *relation*. Whether I turn to a person as a wholly present *Thou* or as an objectified *It*, I exist only in relation to the other. In *I-It* relations, we remain detached from our interactions, seeking to control the beginning, middle, and end, the subject discussed, and how it is defined. In *I-Thou* relationships, on the other hand, I yield my need to control and objectify by fully turning towards and surrendering into engaging the other naturally and spontaneously.

Table 6.1.

I-It Relations	I-Thou Relationships
Never Spoken with the Whole Being	Spoken with the Whole Being
Experiencing/Using/Knowing	Event/Happening
In Space and Time	Spaceless/Timeless
One-sided: Singular	Two-sided: Mutual
Controlling	Yielding
Subject-Object Duality	Interhuman Betweenness

In this light, the central theme of Buber's talk now becomes clear. Buber's own basic stand is a dialogical one. How Buber spoke of his own stand is highly instructive. Often he used the image of "the narrow ridge" between either/or, between subjective individuality and objective collectivism, between conflicting absolute truths, to characterize his dialogical perspective.

On the far side of the subjective, on this side of the objective, on the narrow ridge, where I and Thou meet, there is the realm of "between." . . . Here the genuine third alternative is indicated, the knowledge of which will help to bring about the genuine person again and to establish genuine community.[2]

More than an inner experience, or realization, or transformation, the dialogical sphere of "the narrow ridge," as Buber said, is neither individualistic nor collectivistic, nor the sum of the two. This interhuman realm is a "genuine third alternative" between subjectivity and objectivity. Common to each person, yet reaching beyond their separateness, the relational space on the narrow ridge is ever-and-again reconstituted in our meetings with others, and ever-and-again establishing genuine dialogue.

For Buber, everyone is dialogically constructed (both theologically and socially) and dialogically directed (both verbally and humanly). Further, the divine-human partnership affirms our reciprocal and reciprocating responsibility in life. My stand, my place in the world, is not just a function of my willpower and is not just an attitude of my mind. It also embodies an already-existing dimension, the divine influence of grace that joins with my willpower to affect my presence in the world. When I wholeheartedly and unreservedly respond to the other whom I encounter during the flow of events in my life, without holding back, I am able to become again and again who I was created to be.

Standing exactly where you are situated here-and-now points as well, as T. S. Eliot wrote, in the first movement of "Burnt Norton," "to one end, which is always present." This always present, here-and-now presence embodies, for Buber, being fully "here" in this moment without withholding yourself. Notice that this here-and-now presence is not a singular achievement but rather a presence-for-relationship. That is, I am present not for myself, not just to enjoy life more, but to enter into deep contact with you. Why make such a point of this? Because it is in this here-and-now presence of mutual interaction that God calls us, prompts us, signals us in human language that penetrates our souls. In these moments, the divine sparks (the hidden light of holiness that dwells in each person) are released into the world. In these moments, God's unconditional reaching out to humans reconciles those who unconditionally reach out to each other in a mutually transformational communion.

Taking your stand, for Buber, is always relationally grounded, always relationally directed; taking one's stand is always, in other words, dialogical. One might ask if it is possible to take a stand that refuses to hear arguments or discussion from another person. Buber would likely respond that by refusing "to hear" the other's arguments, genuine two-sided dialogue becomes impossible. A dialogical stand is a living commitment to practice turning, addressing, listening, and responding to persons and to God, to nature and art, to whomever and whatever we encounter. Here there is neither fixed nor final words; here, there is mutually engaging and being engaged by the other; here we glimpse the source of life. For this reason, Friedman writes that "it is precisely through each standing his or her own ground and yet moving to meet the other that genuine dialogue from ground to ground takes place."[3]

HALLOWING DEATH

At this point, the implications of Buber's teaching become profoundly daunting—namely, hallowing death as an integral part of hallowing the every day. One's stand in the world for Buber not only includes our basic attitude toward life, our decision whether to enter one-sided relations or fully mutual relationships, but it also encompasses our attitude toward death. Indeed, Buber offers us a profound insight into death, not through doctrines but through his own life. A few years before dying, for instance, Buber wrote a short poem that ended with a familiar, gentle voice who says:

He who created
You meant: "Be prepared
For every earthy season!"
His hand has ever held thee—
Remain lovingly facing the world![4]

This lyric poignantly expresses Buber's dialogical stand in the face of death: even death, the end of our life, should not change our response to our existential situation.

We have said earlier that by "hallowing," the Hasidic tradition meant bringing an attitude of reverence into everything that we encounter, relating to everything as holy. According to Buber, "everything wants to be hallowed—to be brought into holiness." (OMH 148[5]) This is because for Buber, and for Hasidism, the holy is not an isolated sphere of existence but the realm open to all life. Sensitively and perceptively, Maurice Friedman suggests that "death too is a part of the hallowing of the everyday. . . ." (143[6])

Can you imagine what "hallowing death" (reconciling death with holiness) might involve? How can death ever become holy? Logically speaking, it makes sense to suggest that (1) if all life is holy; (2) if death is a part of life; then (3) death is at least partly holy. But what part of death can be holy?

While studying the teachings of Hasidism, Buber discovered one way which embodies bringing death into life, that is by dying before dying into genuine relationship with life. This doesn't mean constantly focusing on your own physical death, on your final moments of life. Rather, hallowing death involves bringing the awareness of dying into the holiness of every moment, thus becoming more fully alive. Whenever we *turn* fully and *surrender* totally to what we encounter without holding anything back, without trying to possess it, we pass through a mini-death experience. Living with death in this way, letting go of our attachments, projections, even views about who we think we are, we initiate a new relationship with death. In sum: hallowing death means holding/discovering/relating to death with an attitude of reverence and remaining open to its holiness by recognizing God's presence in its midst.

Yet, how? How did Buber manage to affect this counter-indicated behavior? As it was for the Hasidic rabbis, for Buber, too, it is possible to bring death into life, as suggested in two anecdotes that Buber knew well:

> When Rabbi Bunam lay dying his wife burst into tears. He said: "What are you crying for? My whole life was only that I might learn how to die."[7]

And

> "In order really to live," said Rabbi Yitzhak, the zaddik of Vorki, "a man must give himself to death. But when he has done so, he discovers that he is not to die—but to live."[8]

Learning how to die, it turns out, is no different from learning how to really live. A stunning consequence of Buber's stand emerges from another tale in which a person expresses his or her wish, in the presence of a rabbi, to die like a good Jew. In response, the zaddik commented: "Such a wish is wrong. Desire rather that you may live like a good Jew, and it will follow as a consequence that you will die like a good Jew."⁹

A few weeks before Buber's death family members, when looking through his papers, discovered a handwritten manuscript of a poem titled "The Fiddler," which was dedicated to his dear friend Grete Schaeder. A German scholar and writer on literature and philosophy, Schaeder worked closely with Buber between 1961 and 1965 (the year Buber died) in the preparation of her book *The Hebrew Humanism of Martin Buber* (1966). Buber's poem most probably was intended as his farewell to life:

> *Here on the world's edge at this hour I have*
> *Wonderously settled my life.*
> *Behind me in a boundless circle*
> *The All is silent, only that fiddler fiddles.*
> *Dark one, already I stand in covenant with you,*
> *Ready to learn from your tones*
> *Wherein I became guilty without knowing it.*
> *Let me feel, let there be revealed*
> *To this whole soul each wound*
> *That I have incorrigibly inflicted and remained in illusion.*
> *Do not stop, holy player, before then!*¹⁰

Recognizing death's presence in life, and standing in relationship to this presence, Buber's major concern was not to resist or deny death but to seek its assistance. To really learn from death, Buber requests the dark one not to take him until each hurt, each pain that he has inflicted on others be revealed to his whole soul. He stands with death at his side ready to take full responsibility for his life. This poem's incredible insight emerges from Buber's bringing death into life and, in the process, preparing him to die. But again we ask the difficult question: How does Buber practice dying before dying?

TURNING TOWARDS AND SURRENDERING INTO

Two interrelated elements of Buber's dialogical spirituality concretely embody aspects of dying before dying. First is the active practice of turning. True turning with your whole being toward the other is impossible without first turning away from all self-interests and individually oriented preoccupations. That is, genuine turning flows from dying to yourself, so to speak. That is, turning involves revising your normal direction of movement, forgetting your separate self, and un-self-consciously engaging, addressing, and responding to the other.

The second element is receptive—opening up and letting go of whatever you are holding onto. Surrendering for Buber is a special kind of action—action, yes, but without self-referential awareness; movement, yes, but without emphasizing the mover.

> *The [other] meets me. But I step into direct relation with it. Hence the relation means being chosen and choosing, [surrendering] and action in one; just as any action of the whole being, which means the suspension of all partial actions and consequently of all sensations of actions grounded only in their particular limitation, is bound to resemble [surrendering].*[11]

Authentic surrender, letting go of control, occurs only when all self-conscious reflection is temporarily suspended. You'll notice that the surrendering of which Buber speaks does not mean becoming blank, or empty, or disappearing, but rather becoming more alive, more present, more open to interact with others. Turning toward and surrendering into teaches us the art of letting go of the need to be in control of our lives. At the deepest level, just as turning, when genuine, is turning toward relationship with another, so too surrendering, when real, is surrendering into meeting, into we-ness, I *and* you.

I think Buber would agree with T. S. Eliot that dying before dying is made possible by a "grace of sense," by

> . . . something given
> And taken, in a lifetime's death in love
> Ardor and selflessness and self-surrender.[12]

True, these acts of self-surrender require one to risk letting go of one's persona. They also finally involve trusting that in graced moments of authentic engagement the Divine Presence can be realized. That is, dying before dying—spiritual dying—is neither a subjective activity nor an objective forgetfulness. Rather, it is a death/rebirth through which attachments to the self-reflexive, isolated ego again and again naturally and spontaneously dissolve through turning toward and surrendering into genuine encounters. In the process, you too, along with Rabbi Moshe and his disciple, can discover what is most important.

> *Soon after the death of Rabbi Moshe, Rabbi Mendel of Kotzk asked one of his disciples:*
> *"What was most important to your teacher?"*
> *The disciple thought and then replied:*
> *"Whatever he happened to be doing at the moment."*[13]

Turning towards and surrendering into relationship with others is only one way to practice dying before dying. Another can occur when you surrender fully into relationship with God in prayer. According to the Baal-Shem-Tov, a person "should reflect before prayer that he [or she] is ready to die in this prayer for the sake of its intention."[14] Prayer, at least according to Hasidic teachers, is the consummate example of dying to self while yet remaining alive. Reb Uri of Strelisk, for instance, is one who exemplifies the heart of prayer. In fact, it is said that during prayer his soul would travel in celestial spheres where it met other souls. This zaddik took the teaching of bringing one's whole soul into prayer quite literally. As Elie Wiesel, a modern Hasid tells us:

> Praying, for him, was a constantly renewed statement of being ready to die for God. Why did God accept Abel's offering? Because he gave of himself. To pray means to become offering and sacrifice. Unfortunately, said reb Uri, we have forgotten how to pray. We must learn again.

For this reason, Wiesel notes that:

> Every day before services [Uri] put his affairs in order and bid farewell to his family as though he were seeing them for the last time. To his wife and children, he would repeat his last will. To a devoted disciple he would say: "If you do not see me again, remember: the written notes on my table are not mine, but my teacher's."[15]

Consequently, Hasidic prayer—dying to your separate self and into dialogue with God—extends everyday hallowing and deepens our becoming "humanly holy."

How does this insight strike you? Can you imagine what praying in this way would be like? Or do you recognize resistance to the point of this spiritual practice in yourself?

The only way to actually discover if practicing dying while living is possible, and furthermore if that practice makes you more alive, more attentive to the present, is to try it. Thinking about it only gets in the way. If you really want to discover whether or not dying before dying works, practice letting go. For instance, let go of your need to look good and be right. If that is too difficult, select some other attachment to relinquish. You may discover that the practice itself, when genuine, will teach you how to go about it.

What happens after death Buber could not say. But reflecting Hasidic teaching that death is a part of hallowing the everyday, of turning toward and surrendering into life. Buber writes:

*We know nothing of death, nothing other than the one fact that we shall die—
but what is that, dying? We do not know. So it behooves us to accept that it
is the end of everything conceivable by us. To wish to extend our conception
beyond death, to wish to anticipate in the soul what death alone can reveal to
us in existence, seems to me to be a lack of faith clothed as faith. The genuine
faith speaks: I know nothing of death, but I know that God is eternity, and
I know this, too, that he is my God. Whether what we call time remains to
us beyond our death becomes quite unimportant to us next to this knowing,
that we are God's—who is not immortal, but eternal. Instead of imagining
ourselves living instead of dead, we shall prepare ourselves for a real death
which is perhaps the final limit of time but which, if that is the case, is surely
the threshold of eternity.*[16]

For Buber, therefore, it is necessary to prepare for a "real death," the death
of our ego-clinging, monological selves, as a result of which we can be
reborn to God as our Eternal Partner. True, Buber's life-stand maintained
a double posture toward the inevitability of death in life, contending with
death on the one hand yet also trusting in the meaning and value that arises
from our contending. His life-long practice of turning away from self-
isolating proclivities toward engaging the other, and of openly surrendering
himself into genuine encounter continually brought Buber to an ever-new
relationship with death in life. Beyond one's living relationship with death,
Buber says, beyond practicing dying in life before actually dying, "we
know nothing." We exist therefore inevitably in a mode of insecurity. Yet
for the Hasid, this insecurity is not a negative force or demoralizing feeling. Rather, the insecurity is itself hallowed—holy insecurity lived in the
face of God.

BUBER LIFE-ANECDOTE

Of the many episodes in Buber's life that exemplifies the transformative
power of taking a stand, one that occurred on Easter of 1914 stands out. It was
then that Buber met at Potsdam with men from various European countries
to discuss possible ways of responding to the conditions that would produce
World War I. Buber notes that the conversations among these men, intellec-
tuals and spiritual leaders, were "marked by that unreserve, whose substance
and fruitfulness I have scarcely ever experienced so strongly."

In the midst of the discussion, one of the participants, a former minister named Florens Christian Rang, objected that too many Jews had been
nominated to serve on several committees, which he believed would create
an unbalanced representation. Obstinate Jew that Buber was, he raised a

counter-protest during which he came to say, referring to Jesus, that "we Jews knew him from within, in the impulses and stirrings of his Jewish being, in a way that remains inaccessible . . . to you [Christians]." At this, first Rang, then Buber stood up and faced each other. For an intense moment of silence, each looked into the other's eyes. "It is gone," Rang suddenly said, referring to the tension and anger that had arisen between them. Before everyone, they gave one another the kiss of brotherhood. Looking back on this encounter, Buber remarks that

> the situation between Jews and Christians had been transformed into a bond between the Christian and the Jew. In this transformation dialogue was fulfilled. Opinions were gone, in a bodily way the factual took place.[17]

Taking your stand, for Buber, means accepting and affirming the other as a unique dialogical partner, even when you disagree with his or her views. The treasure Buber discovers is the immediacy of togetherness that arises from mutual stand-taking and mutual self-giving. For this reason, when you are fully present here-and-now, the presence of God can be glimpsed. In Hasidic teaching, as well as in Buber's own view, taking a dialogical stand is not only inseparable from glimpsing the God who is "wholly other, wholly same, wholly present" but essential to entering and renewing our relationship with God.

CLOSING TALE

Buber concludes this talk—and therefore his entire presentation—with another Hasidic tale. Once the Kotzker rebbe surprised a group of learned men by asking, "Where is the dwelling of God?" "What a thing to ask!" they laughed at him. "Is not the whole world full of his glory!" But the Kotzker replied, "God dwells wherever [one] lets him in." Buber's comment on this tale is too relevant to the subject of his sixth talk—taking one's stand—to leave unquoted. For Buber, "This is the ultimate purpose: to let God in," and "we can let him in only where we really stand, where we live, where we live a true life."

Why did Buber quote this Hasidic tale? Surely, he had in mind the implied message that the knowledge of the "learned men" actually blocked them from a deeper understanding of God's presence in the world. Learned men and women are competent guides, of course, if one wishes to study the scriptures or the law. But their answer to the rabbi's question does not go far enough to address the existential nature of the question itself. A shift is necessary: from

God as a concept to God as presence in the world; from knowledge about God to engagement with God.

The rabbi who asks the question "Where does God dwell?" knows how the learned men will answer. He shifts the answer from one based in the pride associated with their learning, from one that reflects their own self image, to one that suggests the need to enter a reciprocal relationship with the intention of hallowing relationships in the every day. This tale reinforces Buber's insistence on the primacy of service (*devotio*) rather than knowledge (*gnosis*). God dwells everywhere, yes. Yet our task is to actively let God into the world in the specific place that we inhabit.

If the sixth talk encapsulates the first five while at the same time exemplifying them, Buber's concluding words, beautiful as they are poignant, need to be heard (read aloud!) over and over. He begins with a double conditionality:

> *If we maintain holy intercourse with the little world entrusted to us, if we help the holy spiritual substance to accomplish itself in that section of Creation in which we are living, then we are establishing, in this our place, a dwelling for the Divine Presence.* (176)

These two conditions are flip sides of the same coin. Holy intercourse with the created world releases a holy spiritual substance. We can let God into our lives (1) by hallowing the way we interact with whomever and whatever we encounter and (2) by assisting our "soul substance" to accomplish itself by turning wholly toward others. When we fulfill these conditions where we live, we are establishing conditions for God's presence.

Just as I was finishing this chapter, I encountered Doug, the physicist about whom I have already spoken, at the Health Club. "So Doug," I asked eagerly as he was about to put on his exercise jersey before heading to the main exercise area, "Have you read any more of Buber's book?"

A bright smile greeted my question. "Yes!" he said with an underlying confidence. "I finished it." His face was lit with an inner awareness. "The end is especially powerful," he said. "Very powerful, and it needs to be pondered. Letting God in is a function of what we do in relation to other things. It's very rational."

"There is no place and no time that God is not present."

"But we have to let God in," Doug said. "We have a responsibility. God does not force Him/Herself upon us."

"Exactly," I responded. God depends on us to be let in.

Immediately, as if he had been thinking about it, he asked, and implicitly answered, a question. "Isn't it possible that 'letting God in' also involves 'letting God go'?"

"Umm," I responded as if having just tasted a ripe strawberry. "Yes and no. It would depend on what you mean by letting God go," I said, sitting in front of the locker. "Yes," I said, "if by really letting God in—encountering the holy presence—you first needed to let go of all images, concepts, and descriptions of a third person being."

"That probably applies to most of us," he said.

"No, if the reason for letting God go is because of disinterest, misunderstanding, or anger, then, letting God in becomes what is needed."

Buber's final words indicate the profound sublimity of the Hasidic spiritual path. He concludes his series of talks by raising the hope for all humans that as mutual partners in league with God, we can fulfill our purpose in creation:

> *This is the ultimate purpose: to let God in. But we can let him in only where we really stand, where we live, where we live a true life. If we maintain holy intercourse with the little world entrusted to us, if we help the holy spiritual substance to accomplish itself in that section of Creation in which we are living, then we are establishing, in this our place, a dwelling for the Divine Presence.* (176)

We are responsible for letting God into our lives, to open a space through which God's holy presence can be glimpsed. We do this where we *really* stand, where we live a *true* life. This—letting God into the world here-and-now—is our ultimate life-purpose. Fortunately for us, "God helps with His nearness."[18]

PRACTICE EXERCISES

I. Chapter-Specific Questions

(Designed to bring greater clarity to Buber's central insights.)

1. What does "taking a stand" mean to you? What prevents you from doing it?
2. Buber says that the ultimate purpose of your life is to let God in where you are. How do you respond to this? Do you agree or disagree with Buber? Why?
3. Why did the Rabbi of Kotzk respond to the learned person's remark that the whole world is full of God's glory the way he did—"God dwells where we let God in"? When and how do you let God into your life?
4. What is the treasure that you can find right here in the place where you stand? How do you access it? Describe its happening.

II. Comparative Questions

(Designed to deepen your dialogue with Buber's spiritual techniques.)

1. Now and then a question addresses you with urgency without needing an immediate answer. Looking back at these specific questions, select one that would be helpful to live with without yet having a clear answer. Are you willing to live within the question, so to speak, and allow its echoes, its implications, and its edges to affect the way you relate to the world? What happens to that question when you bring it, unanswered, into your discourse? When is the time right to return to the question and allow an answer to form itself for you?

2. What is the key element of this talk, the central insight upon which the entire presentation is based? How does it challenge you? Imagine yourself in a conversation with Buber about one of these questions which most challenges you or which most surprises you. What do you think Buber would say? In response, what would you say to Buber?

3. Following Buber's interpretation of the Hasidic tradition in this presentation, what practice could you initiate, or intensify, in your life that would embody this understanding? What is the first thing you would do? Then what?

4. What does the dynamic relation between rebbe and disciple indicate about the disciple's behavior? With whom do you most identify in this story? How would you have acted either similarly or differently than the disciple?

III. Feedback Questions

(Designed to help you achieve life-integrations in meaningful dialogue with others.)

1. Select a question from the first two sections that deeply grasped you to bring into dialogue with someone else who has also read Buber's talks. After engaging that question in dialogue with another person, what new insights/understandings emerged from the dialogical interaction?

2. Formulate your own question about the meaning and/or practice of Buber's teaching; bring it into dialogue with another retreatant and record the results. What did you come to realize as a result of that dialogue?

3. Of all the correlations between various responses you have made in your Journal, which one is of greatest value? How have you integrated it into your daily life?

4. Create a dialogue script with Buber in which you ask your heartfelt question and then listen to hear Buber's response as if aimed uniquely at you. In this script you ask a question, and then before answering, listen quietly to allow what Buber might say to form itself in your mind. Later, you may wish to share your dialogue script with friends or family. Notice how subsequent dialogical relationships are charged.

Conclusion

Practicing Buber's Secret

Where I wander—You!
Where I ponder—You!
Only You everywhere, You, always You.
You, You, You.
When I am gladdened—You!
And when I am saddened—You!
Only You, everywhere You!
You, You, You.
Sky is You!
Earth is You!
You above! You below!
In every trend, at every end,
Only You, everywhere You!

—Levi Yitzchak of Berditchov[1]

Buber's first talk captured your attention by addressing you as Adam, as the one whom God asks, "Where are you?" as the one who hides from both the question and the questioner. His second talk reached toward your unique particularity by pointing to the necessity for you to find your own spiritual path in the light of religious tradition or outside of a "religious tradition." Buber's third talk challenged you to pull yourself together in partnership with the divine force, to unify your soul before undertaking your spiritual work. His fourth talk identified the roots of your internal and external conflicts—namely, not saying what you mean and not doing what you say. Buber's fifth talk, seeming to contradict the first four, stepped back for a moment to remind you not to take yourself too seriously, not to set yourself, even your own salvation, as the goal to be pursued and attained. The sixth talk addressed

111

the fulfillment of your existence right here and now, noting that your ultimate purpose is to let God into your life by "maintaining holy intercourse" with the world right where you are situated.

What does all this amount to? Does it find an echo in your heart? The fulfillment of your existence unfolds in every genuine relationship, accomplishes itself exactly here and now where you stand. Your ultimate purpose is to let God into your life, and we let God in—simply and surely—by turning away from self-absorption towards the world, towards others, and towards God as the ultimate source of life. This is the key to each talk: God seeks to become our partner, to participate with us in a co-creative, co-redemptive life. Everything depends on that choice. It's up to us. The choice is ours.

True, it's not easy. But none of us is alone. Each of these six spiritual practices involves the divine-human partnership. Genuinely practicing is impossible without God's energizing grace as well as our directed effort. The partnership between us and God, like the partnership between Hasidism's teachings and methods, is the underlying support of the life of dialogue. The teachings of Hasidism challenge you to practice them, promising results, aligning with tradition, and providing a template for us to fulfill. The practices refine the edges of the teaching, express the teaching's heart center, reinforce its principles, and enact its insights. Finally, the teaching is living event; finally, the practice is living the teaching.

BUBER'S SECRET

The one thing that helps me implement Buber's teachings and practices more than anything else is a special type of praying that I discovered quite innocently one day while reading Buber's little essay "God and the Spirit of Man" in *The Eclipse of God*. While Buber doesn't speak about it directly in his six talks, underlying each of them is his understanding of prayer. Maurice Friedman tells how his chief advisor for his doctoral dissertation on Buber, Professor Arnold Bergstraesser, once amazed him when he asked, rhetorically, "Do you know Buber's secret?" and answered "It is prayer."[2] Buber, however, did not spend hours during the day in conventional prayer. Rather, reflecting Hasidic teachings, he brought himself to everything he did in a spirit of real openness.

But what did Buber mean by prayer? In a powerfully evocative remark, Buber wrote that:

> We call prayer in the pregnant sense of the term that speech of [humans] *to God*
> *which, whatever else is asked, ultimately asks for the manifestation of the divine*

Presence, for this Presence's becoming dialogically perceivable. The single presupposition of a genuine state of prayer is thus the readiness of the whole [person] for this Presence, simple turned-towardness, unreserved spontaneity.[3]

Often, while reading Buber, a phrase, sentence, or several sentences leap from the page with a deep immediacy. In such a way, these sentences have reached from the page into my soul. What had been unclear suddenly crystallized in such a fashion as to be from then on self-evidently obvious.

No longer able to imagine that God's reality and my reality exist in separate and different dimensions, I begin to feel myself participating in an ongoing reciprocal partnership with the God who is ever-present, a God who needs me as much as I need God. Rather than an object of my experience, the God of prayer is the immediate, enduring Presence who can be dialogically addressed (but never monologically expressed) and whose Spirit can be glimpsed in every genuine relationship. It is not surprising, therefore, that Buber would write that when you pray you do not remove yourself from this life but you refer your thought to it, often simply yielding to it. When you are called upon from above, required, chosen, empowered, sent, you, with this your mortal bit of life, are *meant* into genuine being.

RECIPROCAL DIALOGUES

For Buber, prayer is dialogical. While it might seem that prayer and dialogue function in different contexts—prayer in a place of worship and dialogue in everyday life—it is important to keep in mind that the word "dialogue" here does not simply mean two or more persons speaking to each other. When dialogue (whether with others or with God) is genuine—direct, mutual, open-minded, and open-hearted—it embodies and evokes our most uniquely human birthright: communion with God. For Buber, if we use the word "God" to refer to the signs of life that happen to us each day, each moment, we must try

to forget everything we imagined we knew of God . . . keep nothing handed down or learned or self-contrived, no shred of knowledge, and [be] plunged into the night . . . If we named the speaker of this speech God, then it is always the God of a moment, a moment's God . . . In such a way, out of the givers of the signs, the speakers of the words in lived life, out of the moment's God there arises for us with a single identity the Lord of the voice, the One.[4]

This implies, for Buber, that God is always becoming new and that God's presence can never be tied to dogma or ritual. "When we do not believe that God renews each day the work of creation," the Baal-Shem-Tov taught, "then our prayer and fulfillment of the commands becomes old and routine and bored."[5] God continuously enters into renewed, unique relationships with us. Buber certainly had this insight in mind in 1957 when, about 35 years after publishing his little classic *I and Thou*, he added a Postscript to clarify and expand his central ideas. In it, he wrote that God's voice addresses us by penetrating through every genuine interhuman relationship, especially when the words of others stand out as "instruction, message, [or] demand" that we take a responsible stand.[6]

At its deepest level, praying with *kavana* (intention) is an outlook that penetrates my being, a life-orientation that is brought into the stream of living. Praying dialogically does not shut out the world. Rather, it means wholeheartedly entering into reciprocal dialogue with the eternal Partner who touches us with unconditional Love. It also means entering into genuine dialogue with those with whom I engage in the physical world. Genuine human dialogues are inspired by and integrate insights from prayerful dialogue with God, while inner dialogues with God help to recollect and refocus one's outer dialogues in the world. These dialogues cannot be separated. One is a reflection of the other. Praying with all that I am brings me back into conversation with God wherein I address ideas, concerns, and questions and while listening for God's response, recollect words of other partners as if God's response to my prayer manifests through them. Praying in this way enables me to notice God's spirit becoming manifest not only in the natural world but especially as it en-spirits persons with whom unreserved dialogue happens.

Four reciprocal and reciprocating habits of the spirit characterize praying dialogically: turning, addressing, listening, and responding.

PRAYING DIALOGICALLY

Trusting that I am living every moment in the presence of the One who perfectly listens and perfectly responds to innermost needs, I realize how much my life depends on turning my attention wholeheartedly toward God. And the practice is simple. It combines setting aside time (at least a half hour each day) with fidelity to the process of turning, addressing, listening, and responding to God. Once established, the practice regenerates itself.

The reciprocity experienced between these two types of dialogue is contagious. Outer dialogue with others reinforces and deepens my inner dialogue with God: inner dialogue with God reinforces and enriches my outer dialogue with others. Of course, as the Baal-Shem-Tov says, "When we do not believe that God renews each day the work of creation, then our [inner] prayer and [outer] fulfillment of the commands becomes old and routine and bored."[7]

Table 7.1.

Outer Dialogue With Others	Inner Dialogue With God
TURNING • Wholly away from self-absorption by giving yourself to relationship • Toward encountering the unique other as a dialogical partner	TURNING • Wholly away from self-absorption by giving yourself to relationship • Toward encountering the creative Source of life as a loving partner
ADDRESSING • Accepting and valuing this person's expressed stand • Making the other person present as your dialogical partner	ADDRESSING • Praising/adoring/thanking/loving God immediately and intimately • Expressing a question/need/concern vital to your present situation
LISTENING • Attentively, with your whole heart, to what is said/not said • Imagining what the other is thinking/feeling/experiencing	LISTENING • Silently, with your whole heart, for God's "summoning" • Glimpsing spirit-infused signs, instructions, promptings
RESPONDING • Responsibly and honestly without agenda or witholding yourself • Confirming, even when disagreeing, a willingness for future dialogues	RESPONDING • Integrating revealed hints which press inward and stir your heart • Bringing prayer insights/signs into the dialogical immediacy of life

PRAYING ALONE DIALOGICALLY

But if what I'm driving at is true, if God's dialogue with us is fulfilled in our dialogues with others, how specifically does God enter into dialogue with us? How, in other words, can we learn to "hear" God "speak"?

There is no single way of receiving God's address. God's voice emerges in surprising ways and with surprising messages. Every genuine dialogue is unique. God's numinous voice flashes forth from the recollected voices of others, for instance, resonating within the heart-mind of one who attentively seeks, prays, and listens. As the anonymous author of *The Cloud of Unknowing* wrote, God "fits Himself exactly to our souls by adapting His Godhead to them; and our souls are fitted exactly to Him by the worthiness of our creation after His image and His likeness."[8] What really matters is that I enter into the presence of God wholeheartedly, willing to wait attentively without knowing who God is, willing to forget myself.

"In certain moments," Buber wrote, "some of them rather regular, some others just occurring, I am in need of prayer and then I pray, alone of course, and say what I want to say, sometimes without words at all, and sometimes a remembered verse helps me in an extraordinary situation; but there have been days when I felt myself compelled to enter into the prayer of a community, and so I did it."[9] At the same time, everything that Buber said about prayer must be understood in the context of his advice on prayer to members of a newly formed religious community in Israel:

> *You know that I myself do not believe at all in prayer as the objective, as the end in itself. Prayer is a prelude. Study, meditation, fasting, if anyone thinks it necessary for him to fast, are the preparations. But then must come action. Spiritual energy must overflow into social action. Otherwise prayer becomes introverted, narcissistic, sufficient in itself.*[10]

God is the consummate dialogical partner, always the perfect listener who hears every word of our speech and thoughts—even those we are not aware of yet. God completely understands what we mean by everything that we say and don't say, and always responds honestly, compassionately, and justly. And, as Buber wrote,

> *You know always in your heart that you need God more than everything; but do you not know too that God needs you—in the fullness of His eternity needs you? How would man be, how would you be, if God did not need him, did not need you? You need God, in order to be—and God needs you, for the very meaning of your life.*

If we pray, Buber continued, "Thy will be done," we must in truth add "through me whom Thou needest."[11] Impossible to understand, yet necessary to imagine, God needs me for our partnership to flourish, needs me to accept God just as God is ever-ready to accept me, needs me to pray and to listen attentively for signs in daily life, and needs me to live dialogically and relationally. Approaching prayer in this way, my role in praying is shifted. I bear a new responsibility, and with this new responsibility comes a new attentiveness to everyday events, encounters, and exchanges in which the Voice speaks.[12]

CONCLUDING QUESTIONS

After a small seminar I once gave titled "Praying Dialogically," a student asked: "If dialogue is important for getting unstuck from my anxieties and my anger," he said, "what do I do when I am alone at night in a Costco parking lot with no one around? I feel like I need a technique to use."

"If I were there in that situation," I responded, "I would say to the infinitely invisible, ever-present Companion: 'Well, here we are. What's next?' And then I would move into the next moment in that spirit."

"But to do that," he responded, "I would have to avoid going into my thoughts, the stream of worry about this situation or that possibility, which is what I usually do. I feel as if I need a technique to avoid this." What works for me, and it's really the only thing that works, is to make sure that at least once a day I set aside a space of time (at least a half hour) in which I pray alone. Like meeting a friend each day for coffee and conversation, daily prayer solidifies my connection with God's presence. By praying dialogically daily, the practice becomes second nature. It reveals that I am not alone in the universe and that, in fact, I share this life with the eternal dialogical partner. As the Sufi poet Hafiz said, "There are two of us housed in this body" When he awakens, he wrote, he asks God what "love-mischief" can we do today? Here's a technique: stand on your tip toes, as it were, and pay careful attention to God's promptings sprinkled throughout the day's events.

HOW DO I KNOW GOD LISTENS?

Among the most significant responses to this material that I've engaged in came during a conversation with a young woman, Jessica, who said that after reading about praying dialogically she began to practice praying. And then she asked, "How do you know that God is listening to your prayers?" To this she added a second question: "How do you know that God is answering your prayers?" In the context of what I have been saying here, it was as if her questions were influenced by the Eternal Partner. I certainly agree with Buber who, in response to a similar question, once remarked:

> *I know no "objective criteria" and no "methods" in the relation to God. The question "How do you know?" is answered of itself in the personal experience of the believing* [person] *and in the genuine living-together of* [persons] *who have analogous experiences; rather, there it is not asked. I give no guarantees, I have no security to offer. But I also demand of no one that* [they] *believe. I communicate my own experience of faith just as well as I can, and I appeal to the experiences of faith of those whom I address. I turn to those readers who either know from their own experience that of which I speak or are ready to learn it from their own experience.*[13]

The knowing about which Buber speaks here is a dialogical knowing, not just knowing with the mind but knowing with the heart-mind through reciprocating interactions between yourself and others. It is a knowing found in neither one nor the other of the partners, nor in both together, but in their interchange. It begins in a genuine relationship of mutuality, presence, openness, and directness and only then passes over into the categories and structures of subject-object knowledge. In my experience, God is the nearest One who is always ready to become my partner. God addresses all of us directly, nearly, and lastingly.

But doesn't dialogue require each partner to speak? What type of mutuality can exist between humans and God? Even though God cannot be *expressed* as an idea, the presence of God can be *addressed*. As Buber would later write, "True address from God directs [us] into the place of lived speech, where the voices of the creatures grope past one another, and in their very missing of one another succeed in reaching the eternal partner."[14]

I believe that we are dialogically created through speech ("God *said* let there be . . .") and that we become authentic persons in and through dialogical engagements. As my unprovable yet experienced dialogical partner, God is natural and necessary. Thousands of years of testimony from the scriptures of the world's great religious traditions, from the spiritual autobiographies of the saints, and from to the countless reports of ordinary people with extraordinary stories of experiencing the results of prayer attest to this. What once happened to others happens again and again to each of us. How do I know that God listens? Because my experience of prayers being answered over the years by God's unconditionally loving voice continues to perceivably penetrate my history, my biography, and my daily events.

HOW DO I KNOW GOD ANSWERS PRAYER?

God's speaking voice can be "heard" through every genuine interhuman relationship, especially when the words of others stand out for me as insight, wisdom, and challenge. When turning to God with unreserved spontaneity, I bring all other relationships before God to be transformed in God's presence. My conversations with God and God's conversations with me do not only happen alongside the everyday, but penetrate into my daily reality. In event-upon-event, happening-upon-happening, the personal address of God through others enables me to take a stand and to make responsible decisions.

In my experience of praying, life-outcomes do not always fulfill the specific thing that I'm praying for, but they always surprise me in their appropriateness to my total situation. When I frame each day in prayer and then reflect back on the words I've heard, the events I've encountered, and the images and pictures I've seen, insights into God's perspective plumb the depth of my heart. As I ponder these dialogical voices, it becomes clear to me that this is how God gets my attention. God touches me with signs and insights that uniquely address my situation. Something said in a dialogical address with another may, in light of my prayer, direct me to the response that God wants from me.

How do I know? I know in dialogue with you. "Dialogical knowing" is experience-based. "In the infinite language of events and situations, eternally changing, but plain to the truly attentive," God speaks to my heart and hears my response through the language of "actions and attitudes, reactions and abstentions."[15] How do I know that genuine encounters are God-infused? The completion of this book is a great example. *Martin Buber's Spirituality* is the result of countless prayers in which I have asked for and expressed overwhelming gratefulness for God's participation in this journey as a co-author. More than I can attribute to chance—indeed, always—God's voice becomes perceivable in response to specific questions through insights and signs, words and images, gestures and events, emerging through reciprocal relationships. Knowing is finally born of trust, of an unbroken perseverance in my relationship to God's hidden yet self-revealing replies.

Appendix
Dialogue Journal

The coming into being of words is a mystery that is consummated in the enkindled, open soul of the world-producing, world-discovering person.

—Martin Buber[1]

"Reading Buber," a student once remarked in a seminar, "is like running on the beach in combat boots—you get a good workout but it's not easy." For this reason, it is valuable to keep a structured Journal in response to Buber's six retreat talks. I have included this appendix therefore specifically for those readers who wish to extend and deepen benefits gained from Buber's Hasidic spiritual practices. After pointing to the Why and the How of Journal-keeping, and repeating the thirty-two questions used throughout the book, I include several responses to God's question to Adam/you: "Where are you?"

WHY AND HOW?

The Journal provides break-through questions designed to probe the spiritual substance of your life. I deliberately use the word "break-through" in its hyphenated form as Buber used it. Rather than an exalted, heroic, once for all life-change, Buber's concern was with breaking through again and again from habitual routines to dialogical responsibility in everyday reality. These questions, therefore, which emerge from the heart of each talk, are aimed at moving us/you from monologue to dialogue, and from viewing God as not only outside the world but to letting God into the world.

Journal keeping allows you to pause in the commotion of life to recollect, record, and then share spiritual insights, questions, and intentions with others. Your entries, when made with an open mind, open heart, and open soul, and when brought into genuine dialogue with others, provide invaluable directions for the spiritual journey. While narrative writing is the most often used method, you may find other forms more natural, or useful, such as poetry, drawing, or verbal maps. Each exercise leads journal-keepers naturally, and organically, directly and indirectly, into genuine engagement with others. The Journal thus forms a bridge over which we cross back and forth between spiritual *teaching* and living *practice*. The reason for keeping a Journal is simple: it provides us with new maps for the spiritual journey. By recording insights which capture illusive feelings and experiences, it becomes easier to enter more authentically into the midst of your present circumstances.

Writing in the Journal interrupts our routine patterns of behavior and habits of mind. New sensibilities unfold. In the process, we are drawn both farther within, gaining more access to our inner resources, and become more focused and disciplined in our outer engagements. Inwardly, the Journal provides a means of reaching illusive and intuitive insights; outwardly, the Journal reinforces the meaning of our relationships and inspires new dedication for entering them with an open mind and open heart. Fresh insights emerge which we then integrate into our living situations. New connections are made clear. Journal-keeping helps us to discover anew our own uniquely meaningful stand in the world. At the same time, it challenges us with opportunities, as well as new ways to relate to others and to God.

Each person brings his or her own understanding of spirituality into the journal process. Rather than being concerned about the rightness of one understanding over another, we are instead interested in ways of accessing our spiritual resources. At the conclusion of each talk, therefore, readers are given the opportunity to respond to break-through questions, questions designed to draw you more deeply into the heart and soul of Buber's message, to challenge your spiritual identity, and to stimulate new dialogues with other interested persons. One will benefit from recording one's answers to these questions in a Journal, or audio recorder in order to re-read or re-hear these entries later. Exercise questions are of three kinds: (1) *chapter-specific* questions designed to bring greater clarity to Buber's central insights; (2) *comparative* questions designed to help you recognize ways of integrating Buber's central insights; and (3) *feedback* questions designed to put your responses into dialogue with others.

JOURNAL KEEPING

In keeping with Buber's dialogical approach to human experience, *how* we use the Journal is extremely important. Rather than an obligation that we perform resistantly, the Journal becomes like a valuable friend. We approach it therefore as we would approach a person with whom we are in a deeply meaningful relationship. The criterion, in each case, for selecting the exercise-questions is the possibility for breaking-through into genuine dialogue. Being in dialogue with Buber, of course, also puts you in dialogue with the Hasidic rabbis as well as with the tales told. Being in dialogue with yourself, allows you to reflect on different answers that you had to similar questions made at different times in your life. Being in dialogue with others, allows you to reflect on how your insights are reshaped when brought into relationship with another person.

Whether participating in a group or working alone, it is helpful to begin writing in our Journal with an opening meditation. We start by entering an atmosphere of quiet, of silence, without distractions. We sit silently, eyes closed or looking down, breathing calmly. We allow restless thoughts to relax. Our breathing slows and continues by its own rhythm. Body and mind become still. The silence deepens.

With pen or pencil available, we sit in silence, breathing more slowly. Temporarily, at least, we attempt to bracket or suspend distracting thoughts and feelings. In their place, we allow the question to move through our consciousness. We remain open, meditative. We do not write in our Journals until a response to the exercise-question begins to express itself to us. Each time then, we write what, in a sense, writes itself. We do this without evaluating, judging, embellishing, or censoring what is written. When the writing ends, we read it back to ourselves, adding anything that finally suggests itself.

PRACTICE EXERCISES

I. Chapter-Specific Questions

(Designed to bring greater clarity to Buber's central insights.)

Chapter 1

1. If you perceived God addressing you personally with the question "Where are you?," how would you respond? Buber says that everything depends

on how you answer God's call to Adam. Do you agree or disagree with Buber? Why?

2. How and where do you hide out from God? Why? How and where do you hide from yourself?
3. In light of God's question to Adam, ask yourself a question put forth by the ancient rabbis: How far along are you in your life? What have you accomplished? What is yet to be accomplished?
4. Buber says that sterile heart-searching does not prompt us to turn toward God, or toward others, and only makes it more difficult to answer God's question. Do you agree with this assessment? How might turning toward others better enable you to address God?

Chapter 2

1. Name or describe a specific way in which you serve God. Does it differ from your other activities? If so, how?
2. Buber says that everyone should behave according to his or her "rung," or place in the world, which is revealed when you perceive your strongest feeling or central wish. How do you respond to this? Do you agree or disagree with Buber? Why?
3. How does Rabbi Zusya's remark that "any natural act, if hallowed, leads to God" strike you? Does it need to be qualified in any way? Is there any act in your life that has not, nor can you imagine it ever leading to God?
4. What prevents you from realizing and practicing your own unique task in life? How could you reverse this?

Chapter 3

1. Why did the rabbi of Lublin designate the Hasid's struggle with fasting as "patchwork?" Do you agree with him or not? Do you believe that fasting can be a way to reach God? What does Buber say about the Hasid's choice to fast? Does he condone fasting as a way to reach God? Why or why not?
2. What elements of your soul are in conflict? What do you vacillate over? How do you imagine reversing this situation?
3. How do you experience Rabbi Nahum's three rules of checkers—one move at a time; only move forward; from the last row, move anywhere in your life?
4. Do you agree with Buber that it is necessary to unify your soul before attempting any significant task? If not, why?

Chapter 4

1. What is most needed if you are to have a unified soul, that is, "straighten yourself out?" Put another way, how can you find your way from the "casual, accessory elements of existence to your own self?" What is it that prevents you from the straightening? And how can this be overcome?
2. Buber says that the origin of all conflict stems from the fact that "I do not say what I mean, and that I do not do what I say." Is it possible to avoid conflict-situations? How do *you* avoid conflict situations? How do you respond to this? Do you agree or disagree with Buber? Why?
3. When Rabbi Hanokh responds to the "stupid" man's not being able to find himself—"That's how it is with us"—what is he implying first about the stupid man, and second, about you? Where do you look to find yourself?
4. Give an example in which you say what you mean and do what you say. How did it make your life easier?

Chapter 5

1. What happens to you when you are thinking only of yourself? What happens to you when you think of another? Describe the shift from the former to the latter.
2. Isn't Rabbi Mendel's advice—"to hallow your own soul" and "not to aim at yourself"—contradictory? Can each of these statements be true in your life? If so, how?
3. How does the practice of "turning" (away from self-interest toward the otherness of the other) renew you from within? To whom do you turn most easily?
4. List ways in which self-preoccupation prevents you from turning toward God. Which of these would be the most difficult to overcome? Which, the easiest?

Chapter 6

1. What does "taking a stand" mean to you? What prevents you from doing it?
2. Buber says that the ultimate purpose of your life is to let God in where you are. How do you respond to this? Do you agree or disagree with Buber? Why?
3. Why did the Rabbi of Kotzk respond to the learned person's remark that the whole world is full of God's glory the way he did—"God dwells where we let God in"? When and how do you let God into your life?

4. What is the treasure that you can find right here in the place where you stand? How do you access it? Describe its happening.

II. Comparative Questions

(Designed to deepen your dialogue with Buber's spiritual practices.)

1. Now and then a question addresses you with a different urgency without needing an immediate answer. Looking back at these specific questions, select one that would be helpful to live with without yet having a clear answer. Are you willing to live within a question, so to speak, and allow its echoes, its implications, its edges to affect the way you relate to the world? What happens to that question when you bring it, unanswered, into your discourse? When is the time right to return to the question and allow an answer to form itself for you?
2. What is the key element of this talk, the central insight upon which the entire presentation is based? How does it challenge you? Imagine yourself in a conversation with Buber about one of these questions which most challenges you or which most surprises you. What do you think Buber would say? In response, what would you say to Buber?
3. Following Buber's interpretation of the Hasidic tradition in this presentation, what practice could you initiate, or intensify, in your life that would embody this understanding? What is the first thing you would do? Then what?
4. What does the dynamic relation between rebbe and disciple indicate about the disciple's behavior? With whom do you most identify in this story? How would you have acted either similarly or differently than the disciple?

III. Feedback Questions

(Designed to help you achieve life-integrations in meaningful dialogue with others.)

1. Select a question from the Chapter-Specific and Comparative Questions above. After engaging that question in dialogue with another person, what new insights and understandings emerged from the conversation?
2. Of the various responses you have made in your Journal, which one is of the greatest value to you where you are standing in life right now? How might you integrate your response into your daily life?
3. Create a dialogue script with Buber in which you ask a heartfelt question and then listen to hear Buber's response as if it was aimed uniquely at you. Before writing down "Buber's" answer, listen quietly to allow what Buber

might say to form itself in your mind. Later, you may wish to share your dialogue script with someone.

4. Try to notice how your most pressing life-question and the way you have been answering it changes your dialogical relationships with others. What did you come to realize as a result of these dialogues? Record what you notice as you reflect on your meetings with others at the end of a day.

If you have addressed selected questions at the end of Buber's six talks, you may be left with another question: Am I going to continue using the Journal in some manner? In part your response to this question depends on the Journal's value for spiritual living. Recall an area in which journal-keeping has helped you. Be as specific as possible. And then ask yourself if you would benefit from continuing to keep a Journal. If so, what form should it take? Should it continue to be based on the thirty-two questions raised here, especially since not all of them were addressed? Or should you address a question of your own asking? If so, what might your first question be?

To assist you in thinking this question through, consider it from Buber's perspective. Take a question that Buber raises in a chapter and ask yourself not only how you respond to it, but how you think Buber would respond to it? What difference is there between your response and Buber's response? Select a passage (a word, a phrase, even a paragraph) that most engages you with fresh insights or dynamic challenges. Express it in your own words and then enter into a dialogue with it. What would your question to Buber be? Based on your understanding of a chapter, especially in response to Buber's perspective, what would you ask Buber if you could? How do you think he might respond?

GOD'S QUESTION TO YOU

The following are sample responses to the very first question asked in chapter 1: "If you perceived God addressing you personally with the question 'Where are you?' How would you respond? Buber says that everything depends on how you answer God's call to Adam." Each person was asked to record his/her response to this question in a single paragraph, poem, or drawing.

Example 1:

Hiding Out

One day, in the sleepy dark
beneath the rock of my heavy heart,
I heard your invitation. A cool hand,

a gentle stirring like a breeze
moved through the room of my self-pity,
reached toward me, beckoned me
to get up from my chair and to go
into the garden. One by one, I
picked the new lavender blooms.
Like thoughts, gathered them
into a bundle, then hung them
to dry inside the old garage.
Such pleasure to be among the bees,
to gather what I most needed
on this dry and weary day.

—Ziggy Rendler-Bregman

Example 2:

Where Are You Now?

Polarized patchwork. I am grateful for my faith that helped me through my father's moment with God. I prayed for and received God's strength in my time of need. Since then I have lacked focus, feel unbalanced and have been undisciplined.

My M.O. lately has been to try to restore order to my world, although not in conversation with God. I have been busy with many things that were put on hold during his passing. Why? The short answer is that a semblance of order gives me some feeling of control. The deeper answer is that at some level I do not understand death, and conversely I suppose I am still trying to make some sense of life. Some faith! In this sense I suppose I am out of control, since I am not giving it to God.

"Teach us that our days are numbered and to use them wisely . . ." comes to mind. Nothing has ever reminded me of this more poignantly than the death of my father. True, he had an incredibly full and good life. True, death was merciful in that he no longer suffers. At least he is at rest.

Regardless it feels as if my sense of balance in this universe is altered forever, and it may be a while before I regain that balance. Perhaps this is indulgent. The irony is that I know it is God's strength that has helped me through this time, and will always help me through. So why do I feel so distant from my Creator? Patchwork. I have bits and pieces of faith, I speak it relatively well, but I am not living it. I am muddling through. I know He has a purpose for me yet, even now do I shirk from that conversation with Him.

Jim Zenner

Example 3:

Here Am I

In these digital days, or rather, "daze" of dialogical confusion we have stopped listening to our own "inner voice" and, instead, have answered the siren call of technology. We are lost without our GPS equipment, computer programs and cell phones to tell us where we are at all times.

The "voice" that eternally asks "Where are you?" makes itself known when we are removed from our normal, everyday functioning and thrown into a situation we cannot understand or control. Adam hides from God in the Garden of Eden after he and Eve have tasted of the forbidden fruit that gives them the knowledge of good and evil. Abraham, Moses and Jesus lose themselves in the wilderness where they have visions that give meaning and direction to their lives. Also, the countless heroes of pagan and primitive mythology, like Gilgamesh, Ulysses, Adonis, Hector, Achilles, challenge the status quo and are forced to blindly tempt fate when they are called upon.

All of us at some point in our lives must identify ourselves and take a stand for what we believe. That "voice" not only asks us who we are, but where we are. We cannot know one without the other. "*Hineni!*" . . ." Here am I!" answers Abraham when God calls him by name and asks him to sacrifice his son to prove he is a "god-fearing man." Like Adam, as a child and young adult, I was not prepared to answer and so was cast out to find my way.

My family pulled me out of school and forced me to adapt to an alien environment, not once but many times. We moved from one end of the country to another from the time I was nine until I was twenty and in college. Each time I had to re-identify myself and get my bearings, a painful process that was constantly interrupted every few years before I could ever feel truly "at home" with myself.

In response to this insecurity, I developed what James Joyce's hero, Stephen Daedelus, in *Portrait of An Artist* called a "heroic refrigerator mechanism." Normally a warmblooded, passionate creature, I forced myself to adapt to lower pressure and temperature without expectations in order to survive. Along with this came a "martyr complex," a false heroic identity that told me I was born to suffer alone with few friends and little if any emotional support. Consequently, I was always ready to move on a moment's notice whenever my father lost his job and gambled away our savings.

I never really knew where I was emotionally or spiritually till I left home and became responsible for my own direction in life. Over the years, slowly but surely, I have awakened from the numb, semi-conscious state where I could escape a painful, out-of control reality. Now, after seventy years, I feel powerful and confident a good deal of the time. I have finally found my own way as a husband, father, grandfather, teacher, writer and musician, a potent, creative and loving human being who deserves love, good health and success, who is ready at any time to say, "Here am I!"

Dan Phillips

Example 4:

My Response To God's Question As If It Were Asked Of Me

Right *now* I am lying on Mother Earth. The trunk of a sycamore leans above me, a native American style blanket between me and the Earth. A hundred yards east of me is Freedom Blvd. along which car, truck and bus encapsulated human beings are traveling. I have lain here more than an hour. There goes a bicyclist. Perhaps hundreds of human beings have passed by. This is where my body is. My mind has traversed the continent to wander along the watercourse I grew up near. My concern for its wellbeing pulling me mentally into fantasy about how I could have or could now be a protector of it. Human beings build houses in its flood plain, treating its living course as one might treat a drainage ditch. Meanwhile, beyond these thoughts and words, the great force that stands behind all is present. A donkey brays, sound of traffic, smell of sycamore, song of chickadee. The sun has moved and I must move my blanket to the shade. All of this is God's creation. I am in God's creation.

Thomas Miller

Example 5:

God is Asking the Question: Where Art Thou.

The answer to this question is simple and at the same time immensely difficult. I am in continuous relationship between God and the world. Every address of the world with which I mean whatever addresses me during the day, I am also addressed by God. In my response to every address, therefore, I am looking for the message of God to me and to the situation. My response is therefore a form of my dialogue with God as it is my dialogue with the person/situation which addresses me.

So where am I? I am in a conversation with God, humans and situations, which means, that I am in conversation with life. Whatever addresses me, I try to respond to with my whole person, not holding anything back. I surrender to the moment in my conversation with the "God of the moment" and try to respond to the best of my ability.

In my conversation with every person or situation which addresses me, I try to surrender into the dialogue with my whole person, listening and responding while at the same time also listening to God's message to me. So my life is a continuous dialogue of listening and responding in my dual partnership between myself and God and myself and the world. Every moment is filled with new meaning in this reciprocal relationship with the God of the moment.

Mechthild Gawlick

Example 6:

In Your Presence, I am

Filled-to-overflowing with gratefulness that You created me into a correspondent and that You have led me to this particular place in this particular moment;

Right here in dialogue with You, right now ready and open to perceive your Voice as it is mediated through the concrete particulars of my situation;

Endlessly grateful, endlessly loving You for Your unconditional love, for Your ongoing creative, revealing, and redemptive manifestations in life;

Grateful that You are always present, always willing to enter into my life (into everyone's life), that You are my friend, my amigo, my dialogical partner, my companion all along the way;

Acknowledging as You already know multiple failings, selfish actions, and especially times when I don't listen to others or to You attentively enough— "have mercy!";

Grateful that You seek my participation with You in the world even as You continue to advise, to challenge, and to confirm me in the process;

Repeatedly hearing and living with Your question of questions—in its infinitely unique variations—and seeking Your inspiration, Your guidance to shape and refine my responses.

Kenneth Kramer

Glossary of Key Terms

Absolute Person refers to God's becoming "personal" by penetrating our daily moments with messages, instructions, and challenges. As "Absolute Person," God is always new in every situation, always uniquely manifested to each person through signs, insights, and dialogical encounters.

Baal-Shem-Tov refers to the honorific title of the founder of Hasidism, Rabbi Israel ben Eliezer, that is, the good (*tov*) name of God who lived from about 1700 to 1760 in Poland and whose central teaching, which he embodied in his life, was "hallowing the everyday."

Between refers to the immediate presence of unreserved, spontaneous mutuality common to each person, yet beyond the sphere of either, which happens on the "narrow ridge" between either/or, between competing absolutes, where we become wholly and uniquely "human" and glimpse the presence of God.

Buber's "Basic Insight" refers to the dialogical reality that (1) genuine inter-human relationships and (2) genuine divine-human relationships are deeply and simultaneously interconnected to each other and that their reciprocal spiritual energy is redemptive.

Creation refers to the original act of bringing the universe into being by God as the Ultimate Source of life who seeks to enter into an ongoing co-creative partnership with humans.

Dialogue   refers to open, direct, mutual, communication (spoken or silent) between persons who turn wholly toward the other, speak spontaneously without withholding or promoting an agenda, listen attentively, and respond responsibly.

Divine Sparks   refers to the hidden light of God's redeeming presence that fell from the primal creation as holy sparks into covering shells (separating, hindering enclosures) that dwell in each thing, in each person, in each event, and which are waiting to be released and reunited with their Divine source.

Evil Urge   refers to the power of desire that tempts, distracts, and leads us astray, yet whose passion can be redirected to bring one into genuine relationship with others. Hallowing life transforms the urges by confronting them with holiness and redirecting their energy toward holiness.

Faith   refers not just to a conviction, feeling, or belief, but to existential trust that God is always present in our midst whenever we are prepared to go forth to genuinely meet each other.

God   refers to the Ultimate Source of life, the "eternal *Thou*," who simultaneously is wholly *other*, the *mysterium tremendum* beyond all knowing, wholly *same*, manifest through all sentient being, and wholly *present* in this instant and in our midst as the infinite partner.

Grace   refers to the free gift of the transforming, reconciling, and healing spirit that arises in, generates, and supports genuine, interhuman relationships.

Hallowing   refers to a radical shift in one's life-stance that manifests an attitude of reverence for everything we encounter by relating to all things as holy, as wholly present, and by approaching life-events, meetings, people, work with an attitude that opens out toward transcendence.

Hasid   (plural: Hasidim) refers to the "pious" or "devout" member of a believing community who, in following the lead of the zaddik (teacher, leader), desired to live wholeheartedly in relation to God throughout life.

Hasidism   refers to the popular communal mystical movement of East European Jewry, arising in Poland in the eighteenth century (1750–1810), which spans the spiritual wisdom of great teachers, zaddikim, in tales and stories. At once a living reality and a teaching, Hasidism emphasized that God is present and can be glimpsed in each thing and reached through each deed of loving-kindness.

Heart-Searching   refers not just to exploring our heart, but to searching our whole being (body, mind, heart, soul), listening whole-heartedly, and responding with all that we are to questions that God is asking, such as "Where are you?" or "How far along are you in your spiritual journeying?"

Holy   refers to a person, event, place, or thing that becomes whole, wholesome, wholly present, sacred and which, becomes God-infused. Becoming humanly holy happens ever-anew in a living partnership with God.

Holy Insecurity   refers to life lived in the face of God without certainty of salvation, with a deep-seated knowledge of the incongruity of absolute truths, yet trustingly withstanding life's absurdities.

Individual   refers to a self-existing man or woman who puts their own needs into the center of their actions and who relates to the world monologically by reducing everything to the content of their own experience.

Interhuman   refers to the interactive region which happens between persons participating in genuine relationship, to the spirit of "the between" through which a person becomes whole and can glimpse the ultimate source of life.

Kavana   refers to serving God by bringing right dedication, right intention to everything one does by responding to life with one's whole energy, passion, and responsibility.

Love   refers not to a feeling alone, or a psychological capacity, but to unconditional trust arising on both sides of the relationship that deepens, reconciles, and heals each person; love is the responsibility of an I for the other.

Meeting   refers to an engaging interaction, or direct communication between our innermost being and who/what becomes present to us, to the actual occurrence of engaging and being engaged.

Mutuality   refers to the full, spontaneous, and reciprocal partici-
                    pation of each partner in genuine relationship.

Person   refers to one who wholly enters into genuine relation-
                    ships with others, accepting, affirming, and confirm-
                    ing the other as an equal partner while yet maintaining
                    a personal stand.

Present/Presence refers to a double dynamic: (1) being fully "here" in
                    this moment without withholding one's self; and (2)
                    being fully "open" to enter into ever-renewing dia-
                    logue with others.

Redemption   refers to God's unconditional reaching out to humans,
                    reconciling those who reach out unconditionally to-
                    ward others, and liberating those who act with unre-
                    served responsibility toward others. It refers as well to
                    the transforming reconciliation of the whole world.

Relationship   refers to engaging interactions between our inmost
                    being and who/what encounters us, to a close human
                    bonding in which both partners accept, affirm, and
                    confirm each other, and which embodies a past, a pres-
                    ent, and a potential for the future.

Revelation   refers to God's calling, prompting, signaling us in and
                    through natural, historic, and biographical events that
                    penetrates to the depth of our being; neither a fixed
                    body of teachings nor an inner experience, revelation
                    is an ever-new event in which we participate in God's
                    creation and redemption.

Sacrament   refers to the living covenant between the Absolute
                    and the finite awakening in and through all existence,
                    to genuine interactions with the otherness of the
                    other that address and engage you in God-infused
                    moments.

Shekinah   refers to the indwelling presence of God in the world
                    in its present unredeemed state; the human spirit,
                    through one's authentic service to others, reunites the
                    Shekinah with the full presence of God.

Soul   refers to the deepest heart-center of a person from
                    which one responds openly, unreservedly, wholly,
                    and mutually to the world, to persons, places, and
                    things.

Spirit   refers not only to a human faculty, or energy that exists only inside a person but to our deepest relationship to what is beyond knowing, to an always-becoming-potential *between* persons. We live in spirit when we enter into authentic relationships with others.

Spirituality   refers fundamentally to an interhuman, dialogical grace that transforms one from self-centered, self-obsessed individuality to a life of ever-new, ever-genuine relationships between us and the world, us and God.

Standing   refers not to a fixed position, stance, or bearing in the world but to a dialogical openness in the present to whatever or whomever is encountered (e.g., nature, art, music, film, dance, texts) as a dialogical partner.

Trust   refers to a living contact with God who cannot be objectively proved or logically validated; unlike belief in the truth of theological propositions, trust is expressed in and through turning with one's entire being toward God and persisting in a mutual relationship with God's guidance.

Turning   refers to a reversal of one's whole being *from* separation and *toward* deep bonding that opens one to enter completely and unreservedly into the presence of the other, without withholding. Turning is the unconditional response of a person to God's call to enter relationship.

Way   refers to an ever-renewed, unifying life-direction—one's personal path—in which one chooses to go forth to genuinely meet the other and, in the process, meet the divine presence.

Zaddik   (plural: zaddikim) refers to a Hasidic rabbi, the proven one, the holy person, the helper who becomes a respected leader of a Hasidic community by offering comfort, advice, and counsel to believers.

Notes

PREFACE

1. Martin Buber, *Tales of the Hasidim: The Later Masters*, trans. by Olga Marx (New York, Schocken Books, 1961), 281. Buber writes: "We cannot approach the divine by reaching beyond the human; we can approach Him through becoming human. To become human is what you, this individual person, has been created for. This, so it seems to me, is the eternal core of Hasidic life and of Hasidic teaching." Martin Buber, *Hasidism and Modern Man*, trans. by Maurice Friedman (New York: Harper Torchbooks, 1958), 42–43.

2. *Der Weg* refers to the unifying life-direction—one's personal path—that one chooses when going forth to genuinely meet the other and, in the process, to meet the Eternal. It should be noted that the term "Way" used in the title parallels the Chinese term "Tao," also translated as "Way." The Tao, about which Buber also wrote in an extended essay "The Teaching of the Tao" (1909) refers to the cosmic way of all things with which persons must align themselves to be in harmony with the universe. Activity that occurs because of the Tao is not done for gain or with an agenda but rather is spontaneously and naturally enacted. *Mensch*, in contrast to *Mann* (man), is a gender-free term best translated as "human being," or "person." That is, the human way refers to any person who is wholly turned toward the infinite partner. I have therefore endeavored to employ gender-free language throughout this work as much as possible.

3. Although Buber did not explicitly use the philosophical categories of *I and Thou* in *The Way of Man*, they are implicit throughout. To arrive at a comprehensive understanding of Buber's views on religious life, therefore, it is necessary to read *The Way of Man* and *I and Thou* intertextually. "Whereas *I and Thou* provides the conceptual framework for Buber's mature interpretation of Hasidism, the Hasidic tales concretize, through narrative, the categories of his relational philosophy." Laurence Silberstein, *Martin Buber's Social and Religious Thought: Alienation and the Quest for Meaning* (New York: New York University Press, 1989), 207.

4. Martin Buber, *Hasidism and Modern Man*, 49, italics added.

5. Buber's non-dualistic presentation of Hasidic teaching-practice was not universally accepted. Gershom Scholem, for example, challenged Buber's interpretation of Hasidism as being a-historic. From Scholem's viewpoint, Buber interpreted Hasidism through the lens of his "religious anarchism," which demands that humans set "a direction and reach a decision. . . ." Gershom Scholem, *Messianic Idea in Judaism* (New York, Schocken, 1971), 245. Buber valued Hasidism not just because of its historic forms, important as he knew them to be, but because of its power to assist those confronting today's spiritual crisis. Buber responded to Scholem by distinguishing two ways of representing religious tradition: one by focusing on its historic forms (Scholem), and the other, Buber's method of recapturing "the power that once gave it the capacity to . . . vitalize the life of diverse classes of people." Martin Buber, "Interpreting Hasidism," *Commentary* 36, no. 3 (Sep. 1963), 218.

6. Remi Braque, "How to be in the World: Gnostic, Religion, Philosophy" in *Martin Buber: A Contemporary Perspective*, ed. Paul Mendes-Flohr (New York: Syracuse University Press, 2002), 137.

7. Martin Buber, *The Origin and Meaning of Hasidism*, trans. Maurice Friedman (New York: Harper Torchbooks, 1960), 243.

8. Ibid., 254. This purification was necessary for Buber because nothing stands over against, not to mention above, the Gnostic self: "Nothing with any higher right, nothing that can demand of it, visit it, redeem it: the Gnostic redemption comes from the liberation of the world-soul in the self." *Devotio*, on the other hand, is service in the world in partnership with God.

9. Martin Buber *Eclipse of God*, trans. by Maurice Friedman and others (New York: Harper Torchbooks, 1952), 120.

10. Martin Buber, *On Judaism*, ed. Nahum N. Glatzer (New York: Schocken Books, 1972), 145.

11. Martin Buber, *Israel and the World* (New York: Schocken Books, 1948), 186.

12. Taken from a May 1st, 1996 dialogue with Maurice Friedman in an interdisciplinary seminar at San Jose State University and quoted in the Preface of *Dialogically Speaking: Maurice Friedman's Interdisciplinary Humanism*, ed. Kenneth P. Kramer (Eugene: Pickwick Publications, 2011), xxiii.

13. Martin Buber, *Tales of the Hasidim: Early Masters*, trans. by Olga Marx (New York: Schocken Books, 1961), 126.

14. See David Steindl-Rast, *Common Sense Spirituality: The Essential Wisdom of David Steindl-Rast* (New York: Crossroad Publishing Company, 2008), 22, 24, 26–27. Brother Davidonce told me that when he first came from Vienna to Ellis Island he had only his toothbrush and a copy of Martin Buber's *I and Thou* in his knapsack.

15. Buber's talks, "The Way of Man According to the Teachings of Hasidism," can be found as Chapter IV in Buber's *Hasidism and Modern Man* (1958). They appeared later in a forty-one-page book *The Way of Man According to the Teaching* (sic) *of Hasidism* (1950). It is also available as a free download on the Internet. Walter Kaufmann, who translated *I and Thou*, notes that "*The Way of Man* is also Buber's best translated work, but he neither recalled nor was able to find out who

had translated it." See Martin Buber, *I and Thou*, trans. with a prologue by Walter Kaufmann (New York: Charles Scribner's Sons, 1970), 24.

16. "The Way of Man According to the Teachings of Hasidism" in Chapter IV of *Hasidism and Modern Man*, 126–127. In all subsequent references to "The Way of Man," page numbers refer to the chapter in *Hasidism and Modern Man*.

INTRODUCTION

1. Maurice Friedman, *Encounter on the Narrow Ridge: A Life of Martin Buber* (New York: Paragon House, 1991), ix. In an address given at the Martin Buber memorial meeting, Park Avenue Synagogue, July 13, 1965, Friedman said:

> Buber has had a revolutionary impact on the religious and theological thought of our time; his stature as a philosopher is being given ever fuller recognition; through his work on Hasidism he has put before the world "a realistic and active mysticism"; and he is the foremost existentialist of dialogue. Many would agree with the statement that the Italian novelist Ignazio Silone made to the Nobel Prize Committee in 1962: "I know of no person at the present moment who is Buber's equal in the profundity of the spirit or in the power and quality of his expression." Charles Malik, the former United Nations Ambassador from Arab Lebanon also wrote the Nobel Prize Committee, "No living man, in my opinion, deserves the Nobel Prize for literature more worthily than Martin Buber." And he added, "The type of spirit Buber represents could still help in bringing about a reconciliation, in God's own time, between Arab and Israeli."

2. Maurice Friedman, *Intercultural Dialogue and the Human Image* (New Delhi: Indira Gandhi National Center for the Arts, 1995), 14.

3. Aubrey Hodes, *Martin Buber: An Intimate Portrait* (New York: The Viking Press, 1971), 7.

4. Martin Buber, *Philosophical Interrogations*, eds. Maurice Friedman, Sydney and Beatrice Rome (New York: Holt, Rinehart & Winston, 1964), 99ff.

5. Aubrey Hodes, *Martin Buber: An Intimate Portrait*, 56

6. Martin Buber, *A Believing Humanism* (New York: Simon and Schuster, 1967), 117.

7. Aubrey Hodes, *Martin Buber: An Intimate Portrait*, 228. Moreover, Hodes suggested that Buber lived as a Hasidic humanist: his "thought, speech, and actions were fused into one unified life directed toward conciliation and dialogue" (227).

8. Martin Buber, *The Philosophy of Martin Buber* in *The Library of Living Philosophers*, eds. Paul Arthur Schilpp and Maurice Friedman (La Salle, IL and London: Cambridge University Press, 1967), 693.

9. Martin Buber, *To Hallow This Life: An Anthology*, ed. Jacob Trapp (New York: Harper & Brothers Publishers, 1958), 158.

10. Buber was one of the first significant writers to popularize Hasidic Judaism. His interpretation of the tradition stood unchallenged for almost forty years until near the end of his career when Gershom Scholem began to critique it. Rather than Buber's more

interactive relationship with Hasidic tales, Scholem applied a more historical approach. See Gershom Scholem, "Martin Buber's Hasidism" *Commentary* 32 (1961) 305. Buber (as he himself admits) understood the Hasidic texts personally and re-authored them in this re-telling of them. By choosing Buber's dialogic approach here, I echo Hans-Georg Gadamer's understanding that interpretation may be described as "a conversation with the text," from which the reader emerges transformed. See Hans-Georg Gadamer, *Truth and Method* (New York: Seabury Press, 1975), 245ff.

11. Martin Buber, *A Believing Humanism: Gleanings*, 125. My translation of *die Wesensliebe*.

12. See "The hidden spark of Hasidism in Martin Buber's Philosophy of Dialogue" a dissertation by John Taylor submitted to the California Institute of Integral Studies, San Francisco, CA, 2009.

13. With Buber's *The Way of Man* in mind, Ephraim Meir and Alexander Even-Chen rightly assert that Buber wanted to show the authenticity and actuality of a dialogical life as it became concretized in Hasidism. "More than with the past, he was concerned with the living present that may become real in meditation upon an interpreted past. With his existentialist approach to Hasidism he developed a religious anthropology inspired by the Hasidic way of life. In this anthropology, dialogue was the final meaning in human existence. In Buber's personal, selective interpretation of Hasidism, dialogue was the basic characteristic of a movement that led to the renewal of Judaism." Quoted from Ephraim Meir and Alexander Even-Chen's unpublished book *Between Buber and Heschel: A Comparative Study*.

14. Martin Buber, *Hasidism and Modern Man*, 180–81.

15. Martin Buber, *Hasidism and Modern Man*, 49.

16. Martin Buber, *On Judaism*, 80.

17. Martin Buber, *Eclipse of God*, 44–45.

18. Martin Buber, *Origin and Meaning of Hasidism*, 25. Italics are Buber's.

19. Ibid. The Hasidic masters taught that everything contains a divine spark that is waiting to be emancipated. Along similar lines, the interreligious trappist monk Thomas Merton writes: "At the center of our being is a point of nothingness which is untouched by sin and by illusion, a point of pure truth, a point or spark which belongs entirely to God. . . . This little point . . . is the pure glory of God in us." Thomas Merton, *Conjectures of a Guilty Bystander* (Garden City, New York: Doubleday, 1966), 156–158. Like Merton, for Buber, each time I enter into a genuine relationship—direct, honest, open, and mutual—with what or who I encounter, God's presence happens.

20. Martin Buber, *The Origin and Meaning of Hasidism*, 21.

21. Martin Buber, *Philosophical Interrogations*, 68.

22. Martin Buber, *Hasidism and Modern Man*, 58.

23. Ibid., 59.

24. Ibid. Buber's term *der vollkommenen Mensch*, translated here as "the perfected person," can also be translated "the fully realized whole person." The Zaddik, for Buber, attempted to witness to God's unconditional love through acting with "infinite responsibility."

25. Martin Buber, *Tales of the Hasidim: Early Masters*, 4–5.

26. Gershom Scholem, *Major Trends in Jewish Mysticism* (New York: Schocken Books, 1961), 91.

27. Martin Buber, *Hasidism and Modern Man*, 26. Rather than strictly translate Hasidic tales that he discovered, Buber took them into his soul and re-authored them.

I have received [tales] from folk-books, from note-books and pamphlets, at times also from a living mouth, from the mouths of people still living who even in their lifetime heard this stammer. I have received it and have told it anew. I have not transcribed it like some piece of literature; I have not elaborated it like some fabulous material. I have told it anew as one who was born later. I bare in me the blood and the spirit of those who created it, and out of my blood and spirit it has become new.

Martin Buber, *The Legend of the Baal-Shem* (New Jersey: Princeton University Press, 1995), ix–x

28. Ibid., 25. Translation has been slightly altered.

29. Martin Buber, *The Philosophy of Martin Buber*, 744. Remarks such as these take us to the central teaching of the Hasidic faith, what Buber called "sacramental existence," the covenant of the Absolute with the everyday. Buber writes: "Man cannot approach the divine by reaching beyond the human; he can approach Him through becoming human. To become human is what he, this individual man, has been created for. This, so it seems to me, is the eternal core of Hasidic life and of Hasidic teaching." Martin Buber, *Hasidism and Modern Man*, 42–43. According to Buber's Hasidic perspective, we humans have been placed in life with the task of raising the dust to the spirit. In a sacramental view, the holiness of God can be found everywhere. Our task therefore is to respond with heartfelt wholeness to the life-claiming, life-determining encounters we have with others.

30. Martin Buber, *Philosophical Interrogations*, 88, 90.

31. Ibid., 24.

32. Roland Barthes, *The Pleasure of the Text* (New York: Hill and Wang, 1975), 40.

33. Martin Buber, *Tales of the Hasidim: Early Masters*, 107.

34. T. S. Eliot, Preface in *Thoughts for Meditation: A Way to Recovery from Within*, ed. Nagendranath Gangulee (London: Faber and Faber, 1951), 12. For further information on this approach, see my *Redeeming Time: T. S. Eliot's Four Quartets* (Lanham: Rowman and Littlefield, 2007).

CHAPTER 1

1. D.T. Suzuki, *The Field of Zen* (New York: Perennial Library, 1970), 15.

2. Rainer Maria Rilke, *Letters to a Young Poet*, trans. M.D. Herter Norton (New York: W.W. Norton and Company, 1934), 34–35. Italics mine. Rilke continues "Perhaps you do carry within yourself the possibility of shaping and forming as a particularly happy and pure way of living; train yourself to it—but take whatever comes with great trust, and if only it comes out of your own will, out of some need of your inmost being, take it upon yourself and hate nothing."

3. Elie Wiesel, *Against Silence: The Voice and the Vision of Elie Wiesel*, ed. Irving Abramson, volume III (New York: The Holocaust Library, 1985), 297.

4. Maurice Friedman, *A Dialogue with Hasidic Tales* (New York: Human Sciences Press, 1988), 85.

5. Martin Buber, *Meetings*, 51.

6. Martin Buber, *Eclipse of God*, 127.

7. Martin Buber, *I and Thou*, trans. by Ronald Gregor Smith (New York: Charles Scribner's Sons, 1958), 135–36.

8. Ibid., 135–36.

9. Martin Buber, *Origin and Meaning of Hasidism*, 94.

10. Ibid., 136–137.

11. Martin Buber, *Meetings*, ed. and trans. with an Introduction and Bibliography by Maurice Friedman, (La Salle, IL: 1967), 44.

12. Martin Buber, *I and Thou*, trans. by Walter Kaufmann (New York: Charles Scribner's Sons, 1970), 81–82.

13. Martin Buber, *I and Thou*, trans. by R. G. Smith, 11.

CHAPTER 2

1. Buber's view of genuine action is shaped by the Taoist teaching of *wu wei* (actionless action). In Lao Tzu's *Tao Te Ching*, and Chaung Tzu's stories and parables, Buber found a teaching unlike Western views of action. Rather than rational, pragmatic, objective conceptions, *wu wei* refers to unself-reflecting action. *Wu wei* is the absence of purpose-driven activity. Not goal-oriented, without motives, the actionless-action of *wu wei* is spontaneous and natural. Like *wu wei*, Buber's sense of authentic activity involves both choosing and being chosen, action and surrender. Such action for Buber was action of the whole person.

2. Maurice Friedman, *A Dialogue with Hasidic Tales*, 33–34.

3. Alan Watts, *In My Own Way* (Novato, CA: New World Library, 1972), xiii.

4. Max Müller, quoted in *The Bible: Its Origin, Growth, and Character* by Jabez Sunderland (New York: G. P. Putnam sons, 1903), 22.

5. Max Müller, *Sacred Books of the East: The Upanishads* (New Delhi: Motilal Bandarsidas), xiii.

6. This quote is found in the fourth chapter of Maurice Friedman's unpublished book-manuscript *My Friendship with Martin Buber*.

7. Ibid.

8. These two paragraphs are quoted from Maurice Friedman's forthcoming book *My Friendship with Martin Buber*.

9. Martin Buber, *Hasidic Tales: Early Masters*, 38.

10. The advice given in this dream was very similar to the words one reads in the Buddhist *Dhammapada*: "Pilgrim there is no path; you yourself are making it by walking." Quoted in Raimondo Panikkar, *A Dwelling Place for Wisdom* (Delhi: Motilal Banarsidass Publishers: 1996), 80.

11. Martin Buber, *Pointing the Way*, ed. and trans. by Maurice Friedman (New York: Harper & Row, 1957), 109–11.

12. Martin Buber *Hasidism and Modern Man*, 31.

13. Maurice Friedman *A Dialogue with Hasidic Tales*, 43. In it Friedman refers to Martin Buber, *Ten Rungs: Hasidic Sayings*, trans. Olga Marx (New York: Schocken Books, 1947), 37; Martin Buber, *Tales of the Hasidim: The Early Masters*, 66; Martin Buber, *The Origin and Meaning of Hasidism*, 166; Martin Buber, *Tales of the Hasidim: The Later Masters*, 17.

14. Martin Buber, *I and Thou*, trans. by R. G. Smith, 79.

15. Martin Buber, *Hasidism and Modern Man*, 53.

16. Ibid., 59.

17. Ibid., 67.

18. Martin Buber, *The Philosophy of Martin Buber*, 744.

19. Ibid.

CHAPTER 3

1. Maurice Friedman, *A Dialogue with Hasidic Tales*, 81–82.

2. Quoted by Sara Corbett in "The Holy Grail of the Unconscious" *The New York Times Magazine*, September 20, 2009, 41. Corbett's article refers to the forthcoming publication of Jung's leather-bound red book, nearly a hundred years old, that records Jung's confrontation with his unconscious from which dreams, visions, nightmares, and intuitions emerged along with colorful calligraphy, paintings, and drawings of mythic figures and symbols.

3. Martin Buber, *A Believing Humanism*, 148.

4. Martin Buber, *On Judaism*, 66.

5. Martin Buber, *Israel and the World*, 27. God's revelation, God's speech to us is directed and perceived by the whole person. This is why Buber writes . . ."God created for Himself a partner in a dialogue of time, one who is capable of holding dialogue. In this dialogue God speaks to every [person] through the life which He gives him again and again. Therefore [we] can only answer God with the whole of life—with the way in which [we] live this given life" (32).

6. Martin Buber, *I and Thou*, trans. by R. G. Smith, 82.

7. Martin Buber, *Daniel: Dialogues on Realization*, 140–41.

8. Martin Buber, *I and Thou*, trans. by R. G. Smith, 98.

CHAPTER 4

1. See Charlie and Linda Bloom, *Secrets of Great Marriages*, (Novato, CA: New World Library, 2010).
2. Robert C. Morgan is an international critic, curator, and artist who lives in New York City. He is Adjunct Professor of Fine Art at Pratt Institute in Brooklyn, New York. As a critic, he has authored many books including *Art into Ideas: Essays on Conceptual Art* (1996) and *The End of the Art World* (1998). With writings translated into eighteen languages, Morgan is an artist in his own right and has curated over seventy exhibitions.
3. Martin Buber, *I and Thou*, trans. Ronald Gregor Smith, 62.
4. Martin Buber, *Philosophical Interrogations*, 52.
5. Matin Buber, *Between Man and Man*, 40.
6. Martin Buber, *A Believing Humanism*, 50.
7. Martin Buber, *Between Man and Man*, 16.
8. Ibid.
9. Martin Buber, *Hasidism and Modern Man*, 59.
10. Martin Buber, *At the Turning* (New York: Farrar, Straus, and Young, 1952), 44.
11. Martin Buber, *Meetings,* 30–32

CHAPTER 5

1. Martin Buber, *A Believing Humanism*, 144.
2. Buber uses two terms for turning: *Umkehr*, an inner transformation that opens one to entering completely into the presence of the other, without holding back, and *Wendung*, a reversal of one's whole being such that one no longer turns back to his or her self-absorbed self. What *wendung* adds to *umkehr* is a permanent reversal of a particular act of wrongdoing that includes the dedication to correct it.
3. Martin Buber, *Hasidism and Modern Man*, 63.
4. Ibid., 49.
5. Ibid., 64–67.
6. Martin Buber, *I and Thou*, trans. R. G. Smith, 120.
7. Ibid., 116. "*Verbundenheit*" is a German noun somewhat difficult to translate. It comes from the verb "*verbinden*" which means "to wrap gauze around an injury." To embrace *verbunden* toward a person means to bind with them in a closely held and healing togetherness.
8. Martin Buber, *Between Man and Man*, trans. Ronald Gregor Smith (New York: The Macmillan Company, 1948), 14.
9. See Aubrey Hodes, *Martin Buber: An Intimate Portrait*, 9–10.

CHAPTER 6

1. Maurice Friedman, *A Dialogue with Hasidic Tales*, 127–28.
2. Martin Buber, *Between Man and Man*, 204.
3. Maurice Friedman, *A Dialogue with Hasidic Tales*, 35.
4. Buber's unpublished poem included in Grete Schrader's *Hebrew Humanism*, 18.
5. Martin Buber, *Origin and Meaning of Hasidism*, 148.
6. Maurice Friedman, *A Dialogue with Hasidic Tales*, 143.
7. Martin Buber, *Tales of the Hasidim: Later Masters*, 268.
8. Ibid., 291.
9. Lewis Newman, *The Hasidic Anthology: Tales and Teachings of the Hasidim* (New York: Schocken Books, 1963), 200.
10. Martin Buber, *A Hebrew Humanism*, 229.
11. Martin Buber, *I and Thou*, R. G. Smith, 11.
12. T. S. Eliot, "The Dry Salvages," V.
13. Martin Buber, *Tales of the Hasidim: The Later Masters*, 173.
14. Martin Buber, *Hasidism and Modern Man*, 202.
15. Elie Wiesel, "Strelisk," Chapter 12 in *Dialogically Speaking: Maurice Friedman's Interdisciplinary Humansim*, edited by Kenneth P. Kramer (Oregon: Pickwick Press, 2011), 191-208.
16. Martin Buber, *A Believing Humanism*, 231.
17. Martin Buber, *Between Man and Man*, 5–6. Speaking of Rang, Buber recalled what Rang once said about the most difficult time in his life: "'I should not have survived if I had not had Christ.' Christ, not God!" Buber's response indicates remarkable open-mindedness: "I see in all this an important testimony to the salvation which has come to the Gentiles through faith in Christ: they have found a God Who did not fail in times when their world collapsed. . . . (*Two Types of Faith*, 132).
18. Martin Buber, *Hasidism and Modern Man*, 36.

CONCLUSION

1. "Where I Wander You" by Levi Yitzchak of Berditchov (1740–1818), English version by Perle Besserman, found in *The Way of Jewish Mystics*, ed. by Perle Besserman.
2. Maurice Friedman, *A Dialogue with Hasidic Tales*, 134.
3. Martin Buber, *Eclipse of God*. 126. Italics added. This presupposition is destroyed by over-consciousness that *I* am praying and that I am *praying*.
4. Martin Buber, *Between Man and Man*, 14–15. My translation.
5. Martin Buber, *Hasidism and Modern Man*, 191.
6. Martin Buber, *I and Thou*, trans. Ronald G. Smith, 2nd edition, 136.
7. Martin Buber, *Hasidism and Modern Man*, 191.

8. *The Cloud of Unknowing*, ed. James Walsh (New York: Paulist Press, 1981), 122.

9. Martin Buber in a letter to Maurice Friedman (1952) quoted in an unpublished manuscript by Maurice Friedman, *My Friendship with Martin Buber*. Elsewhere, Buber writes that this kind of prayer—a "direct, 'world-free' relation to God"—is called by the Byzantine hymnist "the alone to the Alone." *Philisophical Interrogations*, 85–86.

10. Aubrey Hodes, *Martin Buber: An Intimate Portrait*, 78.

11. Martin Buber, *I and Thou*, 82, 83.

12. Buber's good friend, Abraham Joshua Heschel, spoke about prayer a bit differently: "We do not communicate with God. We only make ourselves communicable to Him. The purpose of prayer is to be brought to His attention, to be listened to, to be understood by Him; not to know Him, but to *be known* to Him." Abraham Joshua Heschel, *Man's Quest for God* (New York: Charles Scribner's Sons, 1954), 10. Agreeing with Heschel's point, which views prayer from God's perspective, Buber also views prayer through the perspective of the *relationship* between God and the one who prays.

13. Martin Buber, *Philosophical Interrogations*, 96.

14. Martin Buber, *Between Man and Man*, 15.

15. Martin Buber, *At the Turning*, 49–50.

APPENDIX

1. Martin Buber, *Believing Humanism*, 31.

Index

149

movement: double, 78–79, 78*t*;
surrender as, 102
Müller, Max, 27
mutuality, 15; definition of, 136;
marriage and, 65; and prayer,
113–14, 118
mysticism, Buber and, xxx–xxxi

Nahum of Rishyn, Rabbi, 50
narrow ridge, Buber and, xxxiv, 98
Natorp, Paul, 12
nature, and unified soul, 43–45
Nishitani, K. J., 43

partnership, divine-human, 13–14; and
beginning with yourself, 57–58; and
likeness of God, 67; and prayer, 113;
and resolution, 46–47; and unified
soul, 45; uniqueness and, 23–24
person: definition of, 136; God as,
10, 14–15, 133; versus individual,
61–62, 62*t*
Phillips, Dan, 129–30
Pinhas of Koretz, Rabbi, xxi
practices: and goal, relationship of,
47–48; importance of, xxxii, xxxvi;
preliminary, 1–52; of presentness,
53–109; relationship among, xxi*f*;
term, xviii
prayer, 111–19; Buber on, 85–86,
112–13, 115–16; and death, 103;
Heschel on, 148n12
present/presence, definition of, 136
pride, 84–85
purification, 83; Buber and, xix, 136n8

questions, xxxix–xl; on beginning
with yourself, 70–71; as challenge,
8; concluding, 116–17; demonic,
17–18; of God to Adam, 5–10–6; on
heart-searching, 18–20; for journal,
123–27; living, 10–14; on resolution,
51–52; sample answers to, 127–31;

on standing here where you are,
107–9; on turning toward others,
87–89; on your particular way,
37–38
quotidian. *See* everyday life

Rang, Florens Christian, 104–5, 147n17
reading, spiritual, xxxix
redemption, 83–85; definition of, 136
reflexion, 78, 78*t*
relation of relations, xxvii, xxxi; and
heart-searching, 5; and prayer, 114
relationship: Buber on, 5; definition
of, 136; versus fear, 25–26; turning
toward, 84; wholeness and, 48
relaxed vigilance, 45–46
religion: Buber on, xxx, 85–86;
enthusiasm for, versus genuine
meeting, 86; issues with, xxv
religiosity, Buber on, xxx, xxxii
Rendler-Bregman, Ziggy, 127–28
repentance, 74–75
resolution, xviii, xxxvii, 39–52; and
turning toward others, 81–82
responsibility: Adam's question and,
6; and beginning with yourself,
59–60; and death, 101; and heart-
searching, 8; marriage and, 65; and
standing here where you are, 106;
and tradition, 31; and turning toward
others, 80–81
retreat, term, xxxviii
revelation, definition of, 136
right way, 31–32
Rilke, Rainer Maria, 11, 143n2
rituals, xxxii

sacrament: definition of, 136; hallowing
as, 33
sacramental existence, 82–83, 143n29
salvation, 83
Schaeder, Grete, 101
Scholem, Gershom, 136n5, 137n10

secret, of Buber, 112–13; and prayer, 111–19
seeking, 14, 69; meaning in, 96–97
self: beginning with, xviii, xxxvii, 55–72; death and, 104; not aiming at, 75–76; straightening out, 63–64; trivial versus deeper, 61–62; turning away from, 73–89
selfishness, 25
service, 25; Buber and, xxx–xxxi
Shekinah: definition of, 136. *See also* God, presence of
Silberstein, Laurence, 135n3
Silone, Ignazio, 137n1
solitude, and prayer, 115–16
soul: definition of, 136; nature of, 41–42; power of, redirecting, 81–82; relation to body, 40–41; unified, 42–45, 44t. *See also* resolution
spirit, 41–42; definition of, 137
spirituality, xix–xx, xxxii; Buber and, 29; dialogic, xix–xx, xxi; Steindl-Rast on, xxiii. *See also* Hasidic spirituality
standing, 97–99; Baal-Shem-Tov on, 24; definition of, 137
standing here where you are, xviii, xxxviii, 91–109
Steindl-Rast, David, xxiii
surrender, and death, 101–4
Suzuki, D. T., 10

Tao, 45, 139n2, 144n1
teachings: on beginning with yourself, 56–57; on heart-searching, 4–5; relation to practice, xviii; on resolution, 40–41; on standing here where you are, 92–93; on turning toward others, 74–75; on your particular way, 22–24
terminology, Buber on, 12–13, 14t
texts, dialogue with, xxxix, 28
theater, Buber and, 68

tradition: Buber and, 28–29; and your particular way, 27–28, 30–31
transcendence, of God, xxiv, xxxi, 13; dialogue and, 65
transformation: beginning with yourself and, 61–62; Buber and, 105; turning and, 77
Trapp, Jacob, xxix
trivial self, 61–62; and death, 104
trust: definition of, 137; and dialogue, 9–10; and prayer, 114; and term for God, 12
turning, 76–77; definition of, 137; double movement and, 78–79; and God, 82; standing here where you are and, 106
turning toward others, xviii, xxxviii, 73–89
turning towards, 78, 78t; and death, 101–4

Umkehr, term, 146n2
unified soul, 42–45, 44t. *See also* resolution
uniqueness, versus imitation, 22–23
Uri of Strelisk, Rabbi, 103

Verbundenheit, term, 146n7
vigilance, relaxed, 45–46

Watts, Alan, 26–27
Way: right, 31–32; term, 135n2, 137
"The Way of Man According to the Teachings of Hasidism" (Buber), xviii; Introduction to, xxii; original titles of talks, xxii
Wendung, term, 146n2
Where are you?, 5–6, 9–10; as challenge, 8; living, 10–14; rationale for, 6–7; sample answers to, 127–31
wholeness, 48–49; elements of, 63

About the Author

Kenneth Paul Kramer is Professor Emeritus of Comparative Religious Studies at San Jose (CA) State University, where he taught from 1978 to 2001. He holds a B.A. from Temple University, a B.D. from Andover Newton Theological School, an S.T.M. from Yale Divinity School, and a Ph.D. (1971) in religion and culture from Temple University. He has published *Redeeming Time: T. S. Eliot's Four Quartets* (Cowley/Rowman & Littlefield Publications, 2007); *Martin Buber's* I and Thou: *Practicing Living Dialogue* (Paulist Press, 2003); *Death Dreams: Unveiling Mysteries of the Unconscious Mind* (Paulist Press, 1993); *The Sacred Art of Dying* (Paulist Press, 1988); and *World Scriptures: An Introduction to Comparative Religions* (Paulist Press, 1986); he is also the editor of *Dialogically Speaking*: *Maurice Friedman's Interdisciplinary Humanism* (Pickwick Publications, 2011).

CPSIA information can be obtained at www.ICGtesting.com
Printed in the USA
BVOW071529031111

275051BV00001B/1/P